How to Be an
Instant Expert

6 Steps to Being
an Authority on Any Subject

by Stephen J. Spignesl

CAREER
PRESS

Franklin Lakes, NJ

How to Be an Instant Expert
Cover design by David Fiore
Printed in the U.S.A. by Book-mart Press

To order this title, please call toll-free 1-800-CAREER-1 (NJ and Canada: 201-848-0310) to order using VISA or MasterCard, or for further information on books from Career Press.

**CAREER
PRESS**

The Career Press, Inc., 3 Tice Road, PO Box 687
Franklin Lakes, NJ 07417
www.careerpress.com

Library of Congress Cataloging-in-Publication Data

Spignesi, Stephen J.
    How to be an instant expert : 6 steps to being an authority on any subject / by Stephen
  J. Spignesi.
        p.   cm.
    Includes index.
    ISBN 1-56414-476-3
    1. Expertise—Research—Methodology.   I. Title.

    BF378.E94 S68   2000
    808'.02—dc21   00-057942

Dedication

This one is for my beloved cousins, Gayze and Judi, two of my biggest fans and a source for me of much love and support ever since they were ten years old. (I was not around before then.)

Contents

What Is an Instant Expert?

> **When you stop learning, stop listening, stop looking and asking questions, always new questions, then it is time to die.**
>
> **—Lillian Smith**

What is an instant expert? Well, an instant expert is someone who must learn a great deal about a subject in a relatively short time (usually under a deadline of some sort), in order to write something about that subject.

The purpose of this book is to help you find what you need to know so that you can write your book, magazine article, speech, or term paper, presenting yourself as an authority on the subject—no matter how narrow the parameters of your topic may be.

The whole point of this process is that you must come across as an expert on your subject if you want people to take you seriously, be they your readers, listeners, or professors.

Okay, "instant" may be a misnomer, or at least a tad of an exaggeration. All quality research takes time, effort, and focus; so, instead, let's interpret the word "instant" to mean "without wasting time."

My hope with this book, however, is to do more than just steer you in the right direction to find the right facts in

a prompt and efficient manner. I will also show you how to structure your work, interpret your materials, and create your own "voice," all of which will hopefully result in an entertaining and informed work. (Or, more to the point, one that will produce significant royalties, healthy magazine sales, a standing ovation, or an excellent grade!)

This process is a six-step system that will hopefully help you develop a writer's skills. The steps are:

1. Immersion.
2. Notes.
3. Review and Think.
4. Table of Contents.
5. Chapter by Chapter.
6. Review and Polish.

I have found some of the "research guides" that are currently available in the bookstores to be more work than I have time for. Some of these tomes are enormous. By the time I find what I'm looking for *in the book*, I often do not have the time to go find the information I need.

How to Be an Instant Expert can be read in its entirety before doing any writing whatsoever. The art of crafting a readable, well-researched piece is discussed at length in this book because all the research materials in the world are not worth a plugged nickel if you do not know how to put them to good use.

So, to sum up, you are faced with the task of having to write something. You have to write something about which you do not know a great deal.

Congratulations! You've come to the *write* place.

Stephen J. Spignesi
New Haven, CT
June 1, 2000

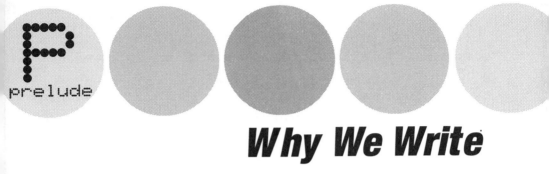

Why We Write

> **_Tenet insanabile multos scribendi cacoethes._**
> **(Many suffer from the incurable disease of writing.)**
>
> —**Juvenal**

The following is an excerpt from *Shelter Street*, a novel-in-progress I have been working on for several months. I am including it here because the speech by the main character, a legendary novelist named Lennon Blake, seems to me to be the essence of why writers write. (Well, this writer anyway.) As a way of beginning this effort of ours, I hope you find this brief fictional prelude useful and inspiring.

●●●

Karen is attending a literature class taught by the acclaimed writer, Lennon Blake, author of *Band Camp*, one of the biggest best-sellers in publishing history and a literary phenomenon unlike anything written in the 20th century. Karen is awestruck just being in the presence of Blake and hangs on his every word. In this scene, she is about to experience the magic that words can weave as Blake talks about why he wrote his magnum opus.

"Writing for a living is a horrid way to live your life. And yet if writing is your calling, then it is as necessary as eating. And sleeping. And breathing."

Karen realized she was holding her breath. In no time at all, Lennon Blake had completely captivated his young charges—precisely as he had done with *Band Camp*.

In fact, the first few paragraphs of that astonishing novel usually were all someone needed to read to stop whatever else they were doing and finish the book in one white-hot read. There was a joke going around for a time that Blake's publishers, at the request of bookstore owners, were thinking about recalling the millions of copies of *Band Camp* in stores so they could shrink-wrap them and thus prevent readers from starting the book standing up in a store and spending hours turning pages feverishly to finish the book without buying it! It wasn't true, but there were many bookstore browsers who made the mistake of reading the first couple of pages and then not being able to pull themselves away from Blake's gripping tale. Most of these hapless souls ended up buying the book and spending the rest of the day and much of their evening reading it.

"Yes?"

Karen's reverie was interrupted by Lennon Blake taking a question from a pimply girl with long red hair three rows in front of her.

"I hope you don't mind me asking, Professor Blake, but what were your intentions when you started writing *Band Camp*?"

Lennon Blake smiled. And sighed. The question. It always came. He had resigned himself to answering it and had developed a lyrical summary of what he went through writing *Band Camp*. How much of it was true he still had not yet determined. But it did seem to strike a chord in those who heard it.

"What were my intentions? Ah, my dear girl...you want a peek behind the curtain, don't you? You want to see the Wizard, right? You want a glimpse of the priest donning his robes...you want to see the zeros and ones that make up the magical code that allowed me to write *Band Camp*, don't you?"

The girl blushed, smiled, and nodded enthusiastically.

"Well, okay," Blake said to her, "you asked for it. And may God have mercy on your souls."

The class laughed and settled themselves more comfortably into their seats. They had all heard rumors of Blake's "Why I Wrote *Band Camp*" exegesis, but none of them had ever dreamed they'd hear it on the first day of class.

Lennon Blake walked to the corner of the lecture hall where there stood a desk chair with arms. He picked it up, carried it over to the center of his lecture stage and placed it in front of the lectern.

Blake sat down, pulled a cigarette out of a pack in his shirt pocket, put it in his mouth, and crossed his left leg over his right. He did not light the cigarette. Blake closed his eyes for a few seconds, removed the cigarette from between his lips and began to speak.

"I wanted it to be a big book.

"I wanted it to be the kind of book that's bound in leather and has Bible paper and small type filling the pages.

"I wanted it to be something you dip into; something that you carry around with you; something that you keep by your side at all times.

"I wanted this book to be the kind of book that has a satin bookmark sewn right into the binding.

"I wanted this book to be the most important thing in your life.

"I wanted you to feel comforted simply holding it and thrilled every time you opened it up.

"I wanted to write a book that you would thank me for writing.

"I wanted reading this book to be like doing the greatest drug ever concocted. Imagine heroin, cocaine, marijuana, alcohol, and mescaline all combined into a perfectly balanced chemical compound that would keep you euphoric, calm, focused, and creative 24/7—that's what I wanted *Band Camp* to do to you.

"I wanted this book to be the world's biggest best-seller.

"I wanted it to win a Nobel Prize and a Pulitzer Prize and a National Book Award.

"I wanted world-famous authors to e-mail me sycophantic messages.

"I wanted the President of the United States to mention this book at a press conference.

"I wanted Oprah to name my book as one of her book club choices and then put an end to the club because no book would be worthy to be picked after mine was selected.

"I wanted you to buy this book for all your friends and family members because you could not live another moment in peace knowing that they did not have it in their possession.

"I wanted this book to be on every magazine cover and in every store in the world.

"I wanted this book to outsell the Bible in every language.

"I wanted this book to be sold everywhere and to have such an enormous and beloved presence in the world that people everywhere would smile when they walked by a window in which it was displayed and saw its stark white cover.

"I wanted legends and myths and rumors to spring up about me, the brilliant yet tortured and reclusive author of this incredible book.

"I wanted me and my book to be the subject of dozens of Internet newsgroups and thousands of worshipful fan Web sites.

"I wanted this book to be translated into every single language on the planet, including Esperanto.

"I wanted the publication of *Band Camp* to be the most important event in the history of civilization.

"I wanted animals to suddenly evolve to a higher state so that they would be able to read this book; and I wanted them to know that the reason they must immediately step on the evolutionary gas pedal is because every minute that goes by that they cannot read is a minute that they are not reading *Band Camp*.

"I wanted wars to end after the two warring sides read my book.

"I wanted the hole in the ozone layer to repair itself after reading my book.

"I wanted Jesus Christ himself to return to Earth just so he could get a signed copy of my book.

"I wanted trees to grow eyes so they could read my book.

"I wanted sea creatures to breathe oxygen so they could leave the sea. I wanted oceans to grow bridges so these creatures could get to a bookstore."

Lennon Blake paused.

"And that's why I wrote *Band Camp*."

Lennon Blake put his unlit cigarette in his mouth, rose, returned the chair to the corner, and walked to his lectern. Throughout these few moments, the room was quiet enough so that everyone could hear the writer's shoes on the wooden floor as he walked.

section I

Six Steps, Seven Questions

chapter 1

The Proper Placement of Bathroom Fixtures

> *When you're writing, you're trying to find out something which you don't know.*
>
> —James Baldwin

The first thing I remember writing was a 10-page short story that I proudly (and naively) described as a "spy satire." I was 11 years old and I printed my story on looseleaf paper with a blue ballpoint pen. I showed the piece to my mother, and she read it with enthusiasm. But, she gently suggested to me that satire usually required a certain ironic worldview that may not be part of an 11-year-old's sensibility. (God bless all the mothers of budding artists...and musicians...and writers, for their ubiquitous, good-humored patience.)

Rather than discouraging me, this actually spurred me to write *more* (after I looked up the word "ironic" in the dictionary, of course). Instead, I began to write about what I knew—or could learn about—instead of things of which I had no real understanding.

This episode was a revelation to me, although "write what you know" is the first thing budding writers read or are told when they begin to pursue what can justifiably be described as an elusive art.

Many acclaimed writers have weighed in on the "write what you know" advice and I have always felt that one of the wisest pearls of wisdom was the following comment by novelist E. L. Doctorow:

> *Writing teachers invariably tell students, "Write about what you know." That's, of course, what you have to do, but on the other hand, how do you know what you know until you've written it? Writing is knowing. What did Kafka know? The insurance business. So that kind of advice is foolish, because it presumes that you have to go out to a war to be able to do war. Well, some do and some don't. I've had very little experience in my life. In fact, I try to avoid experience if I can. Most experience is bad.*

What Mr. Doctorow is telling us here is that writers are much more than simple chroniclers of "what they know." The people who compile the bathroom fixture catalog for the local hardware store are telling us what they know about toilets and sinks, but you sure as hell wouldn't call it "writing."

No, a writer is a channel, an interpreter, and a filter. An individual writer's unique perception; his or her individual spin on a subject, a person, an event, is what creates art. This is what people pay for when they buy a book or a magazine with work written by that certain someone or they attend a lecture by that person. They want to know what *that* writer thinks about a certain subject and how he or she interprets it. They don't just want a listing of the bathroom fixtures—they want to know why a certain type of fixture belongs in a certain type of bathroom and why it would be wrong to put it someplace else. They want to understand.

The key to effective nonfiction writing is this: You do not want to simply give a reader information. To do so is a betrayal of the art of writing. You want to help a reader understand the subject. However, to do that, you need to know what you are writing about. And to do that, you need to know how to find the information you need, so that you can know what you are writing about.

Once you are well-versed in your subject—or more to the point, *only* after you are well-versed in your subject, can you then interpret the facts and information through your own unique sensibility and, in the end, hopefully create art. Art that enlightens. Art that teaches. And art that, of course, *entertains*. And that's where this book comes in: To help you find the right path through a dark and often confusing wood.

But it is also my hope that this book will be more to you than just a hands-on guide to doing research for a writing project.

The writing of the work itself will also be addressed and we will suggest effective ways of expressing yourself within the context of your project. Chapter 21, titled "34 Rules to Write By" gives some down-and-dirty tips, suggestions, and facts about writing as a full-time career, or writing on a freelance basis.

In Hollywood, the more jaded (or more realistic) participants in the machinery of the movie industry often say, "It's not called 'show friendship'...it's called 'show *business*.'" This also applies to the publishing industry.

I have often advised beginning writers that they need to be two people: the artist and the marketer. The artist creates the story, book, article, screenplay, song, poem, play, whatever. The marketer *sells* them. These are two distinctly different efforts and they will never meet in the middle.

You cannot write for money; you must write for yourself. But then when you try and sell your work, you must put on a different hat and convince an editor, producer, magazine publisher, record company, etc., that others will be interested enough in your creation to pay money to experience it.

This is the cold, hard truth: The powers-that-be in the world of the arts are more used to seeing crap than excellence; thus, they are more prone to quickly reject something than to embrace it.

Your role in this equation is to, first, not create crap (which is easier said than done); and second, refuse to take no for an answer if you're certain that what you have created has merit, entertainment value, and marketability.

> **"** *One great inhibition and obstacle to me was the thought: Will it make money? But you find that if you are thinking of that all the time, either you don't make money because the work is so empty, dry, calculated and without life in it. Or you do make money and you are ashamed of your work."*
>
> **—Brenda Ueland**

My first book, *Mayberry, My Home Town*, was rejected by 28 publishers before I sold it. It was eventually published in 1987 and is still in print. Why? Because I knew it was a terrific book and I *refused* to take no for an answer. I believed in it.

Today, I have been writing for more than 30 years, and I am into my second decade of earning my living as a full-time writer. My books are on a wide range of historical and popular culture subjects: from American history to horror films.

Believe me when I tell you that some of these topics were so unknown to me that I had to start at the very beginning to write about them confidently. I knew nothing about V.C. Andrews or the *Gone With the Wind* phenomenon when these books were offered to me. Yet, I ended up writing books about these topics that are now considered definitive. How? One of the results of writing so many nonfiction books in such short periods of time (always with pressing deadlines) is that I have developed a sure-fire system for becoming an instant expert on any subject with clarity and authority. These steps are:

1. **Immersion:** Find out as much as possible about your subject, to the point of almost being overwhelmed with information.
2. **Notes:** Find the diamonds in the heaps of rough data you have compiled and then select the best.
3. **Review and Think:** Step back, mull over what you have learned, and rethink your original vision for your product.
4. **Table of Contents:** Bring order to chaos. Structure your work—and see it for the first time with a beginning, middle, and end.
5. **Chapter by Chapter:** Time to pull everything together and write.
6. **Review and Polish:** Now, after a long pause, we rewrite.

You need to recognize what you need to know to write effectively about your subject, find that information quickly, process the information and retain what is valuable, and then execute the writing process itself.

It is difficult to be specific when you must be vague. I do not know what you will be writing about. I have no clue as to the project to which you will apply my techniques. I cannot begin to imagine the piece you will write, but hopefully, you will make good use of the suggestions and the detailed examples scattered throughout this book.

There Is No Spoon

Mr. Clemens is right: Getting the facts straight first is the paramount goal of all writers—especially for nonfiction writers. What you choose to do with the facts after you uncover them is up to you. It is this process of interpretation that makes each writer's vision so unique.

Over the years, I wasted a great deal of time and encountered far too many dead ends doing futile and pointless research. Through trial and error, I developed an effective system to get to the information I needed as quickly and as efficiently as possible.

This system will not work for every research situation. However, for the nonfiction book writer, magazine article writer, speaker, or student, this system can be applied to most of your needs quite effectively.

If you follow the general principles of this approach, you should be able to zero in on what you need to know and to write your project with interesting and informative results.

This system will not teach you how to write, though. In fact, I'm not even sure writing *can* be taught (all of

the writing classes, books about writing, and magazines for writers notwithstanding). A natural born writer is wired differently. Yet, writing does not have to be an innate calling in order for you to be able to do research effectively and write effective prose based on your research.

A writer needs to always be an observer, to always be watching, no matter what his or her level of participation is in a given situation.

Writers notice things other people are oblivious to…such as that move women make when they are carrying a pocketbook with a shoulder strap. You know the one: A woman needs to bend over to look in a showcase in a store or pick something up off the floor and, as they bend, they push their pocketbook behind them to prevent it from falling off their shoulder. It's an automatic gesture and just about every woman does it.

Or the way your boss unconsciously hooks his right thumb in the waistband of his pants, but only when he's smoking a cigarette with his right hand.

Or how your 6-year-old daughter arranges her food so that her peas don't touch her mashed potatoes...just like her mother does.

Or the way David Letterman grabs the arm of the chair his guest is seated in before he goes to a commercial...but only if he and his guest have had an especially engaging conversation in the previous few minutes.

Or how your cat will circle his litter box three times before getting in and using it. Or how his ears can move independently of each other and swivel to face sounds coming from different directions at the same time.

Writers notice these things.

I am not saying that "literary civilians" are not also aware of these affectations, quirks, mannerisms, and other tropes and characteristics of people. They most certainly are. But writers mentally store these moments in their minds and will deliberately try and find a way to use them in their writing.

I was recently told a story (a *true* story) about a restaurant owner who defrosted his frozen shrimp on top of a dumpster behind his restaurant; and hung frozen salmon fillets on a clothesline strung between two discarded shoe display racks. You can't buy images like that and I am just waiting for the right chance to use them. (And they are mine, so hands off!)

This enduring awareness, this constant posture of watchfulness, this relentless pursuit of the sociocultural singularities of the human condition and of the writer's experience of reality, is, at its core, nothing more than getting the facts straight.

Whether you are writing fiction or nonfiction, you must be honest in depicting your vision of the world you are writing about at all times.

And what is most effective about understanding these techniques and then applying them to your own projects is that they can be taught. You do *not* need to be the aforementioned natural born writer to train yourself to think like one.

Our subject could be 18th-century France; prehistoric Africa; 21st-century Silicon Valley; 2nd-century Jerusalem; the confines of an airplane

> **66** *Do not try and bend the spoon. That is impossible. Only try and realize the truth: There is no spoon."*
> **—One of the Potentials in** *The Matrix*

flying to Denmark; an elevator in the Maritime Building on Long Wharf in New Haven, Connecticut; or the offices of the busiest real estate firm in Portland, Oregon. If you are writing about any of these subjects, or the countless others available to the writer with an attentive eye, then you will need to get the facts straight.

Of course, personal observance and participation can also play an important role in ascertaining the truth of a milieu or of an environment. Unless you have a time machine, visiting Victorian England isn't going to happen. However, you *can* do the research to learn what you need to know, and hopefully create a base of knowledge that you can then refer to when necessary, and dip into when your project so compels you.

I will now move on to a discussion of how to define your subject (there's more to it than just coming up with a title!) and the value, necessity, and magic of specificity.

The Six Steps:
An Introduction

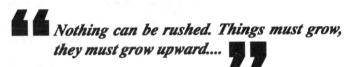

Nothing can be rushed. Things must grow,
they must grow upward....

—Paul Klee

journey is always easier with a map. The Six Step System will serve as the map of your writing expedition. By following it carefully, you should be able to create your project in a systematic, logical fashion.

I have mentioned individual steps of our research process earlier throughout this volume, but now let's look at the six steps process in its entirety.

To review, the six steps are:

1. **Immersion.**
2. **Notes.**
3. **Review and Think.**
4. **Table of Contents.**
5. **Chapter by Chapter.**
6. **Review and Polish.**

We will discuss each step in detail in its individual section, but let's take a quick look at what our goals are and how each step will assist us along the way.

Step 1: Immersion

This first step involves immersing yourself in your subject, almost to the point of being overwhelmed. After all, how can you get wet if you don't dive in

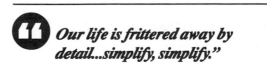 *Artists can color the sky red because they know it's blue. Those of us who aren't artists must color things the way they are or people might think we're stupid."*

—Jules Feiffer

the water? This step requires no writing whatsoever, but rather *lots* of reading (and perhaps some phone calls to knowledgeable sources) as you intensely immerse yourself in your subject. You will learn how to use search engines, what to print out and what to ignore, what to photocopy and what to skip over, what to highlight, and how to selectively scan books for the right information. Helpful insider tips will steer you in the right direction.

For example, if you were given the assignment of writing an article about Chinese food, you could collect takeout menus from all the Chinese restaurants in your area. In one afternoon, you will have instantly acquired a gold mine of valuable research materials. Once all of these sources have been read or scanned, and the researcher begins to feel a strong familiarity with the subject, it's time to take notes.

Step 2: Notes

This step guides you through the preliminary note-taking process, in which you begin putting down on paper random

Our life is frittered away by detail...simplify, simplify."

—Henry David Thoreau

thoughts, phrases, questions, images, and other ideas related to your subject that will act as the foundation for your article, book, paper, speech, etc.

Step 3: Review and Think

Step 3 is a step back, so to speak. At this stage, you will review your materials and your notes again, and think about what to

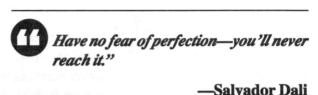

Have no fear of perfection—you'll never reach it."

—**Salvador Dali**

leave in and what to throw out. You will learn how to use your newly informed sense of your topic and refine your database down to only those materials and notes that will help you fulfill your vision of the project. Once this review has been completed and you have a strong sense of what you want to cover in your project, you will begin the first real writing— the creation of the table of contents of your work.

Step 4: Table of Contents

Begin at the beginning. The term "table of contents" usually refers to the contents of a book, but my

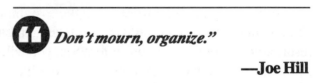

Don't mourn, organize."

—**Joe Hill**

six step system uses it in a broader context. Step 4 will teach you how to draft a detailed outline of your work, in what order to cover your material, and how to structure a coherent, logical work that accurately covers your subject.

Step 5: Chapter by Chapter

Let the writing begin! This step will show you how to write each chapter (or section) of your work with confidence, using your notes, materials, and other sources.

Step 6: Review and Polish

Even Hemingway and Faulkner did second drafts, so don't get too attached to your first draft (which, hopefully, was completed in Step 5). Step 6 discusses the polishing, revising, and improve-

 The advice that means the most to me right now was not delivered directly to me. It's something I read that Fred Astaire said about his dance routines: "Get it 'til it's perfect, then cut two minutes."

—**Susan Stamberg**

ments that can be made to your work before submission or presentation. You'll find helpful tips on formatting, spell-checking, word counts, and many other aspects of putting the finishing touches on anything from a 100,000-word book to a 5-minute mini-speech.

On allocating your time

If you try to divvy up your time accordingly, your project should become a reality in due time. When using the Six Step Sys-

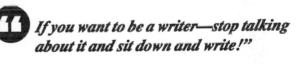 *If you want to be a writer—stop talking about it and sit down and write!"*

—**Jackie Collins**

tem, I suggest the following allocation of your time and efforts:

- Immersion, 25 percent.
- Notes, 20 percent.
- Review and Think, 10 percent.
- Table of Contents, 10 percent.
- Chapter by Chapter, 25 percent.
- Review and Polish, 10 percent.

Now let's get started!

chapter

In the Beginning

n the beginning, the first thing you must do is define your subject. And the key word in that mandate is define.

The great American poet and writer Carl Sandburg asks in volume 1 of *The War Years*, his classic multivolume biography of Abraham Lincoln, "How and why did men and women do what they did? And how can we be sure they did what the record may seem to show they did?" Sandburg's conclusion?

"The teller does the best he can and picks what is to him plain, moving, and important—though sometimes what is important may be tough reading, tangled, involved, sometimes gradually taking on interest, even mystery, because of the gaps and discrepancies."

Carl Sandburg is very well-known for his poetry. He worked with the American popular idiom, yet he brought a poet's sensibility to his use of language, often elevating the simple to the transcendent and doing it effortlessly.

Sandburg's classic poem "Grass" exemplifies this. Throughout the brief

poem, we hear the mournful refrains of the grass: "I am the grass; I cover all," "Shovel them under and let me work," and "I am the grass. Let me work." The poem brings grass to life, specifically the grass that covers the graves of the war dead. In this way, grass becomes a symbolic blanket that *literally* speaks for itself.

Along the same vein, in Sandburg's poem "Broken-face Gargoyles" death speaks directly to the reader. The effect is hypnotic in its approach:

> *All I can give you is broken-face gargoyles.*
> *It is too early to sing and dance at funerals...*

No question about it: Carl Sandburg was a gifted poet. But Sandburg wrote much more than poetry, and his other occupations and avocations explain why the subjects of both his poetry and nonfiction are so well-defined, clear, and specific.

During his life, Carl Sandburg was a migratory laborer, a milkman, a harvest hand, a stage hand, a barbershop porter, a brickmaker, a sign painter, a hotel dishwasher, a salesman, and, most importantly, a roving newspaper reporter.

Reporters must get the facts straight. They must be totally accurate at all times and must always be

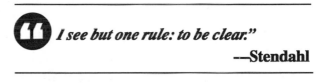

"*I see but one rule: to be clear.***"**
—Stendahl

writing about a specific subject—whether it's a politician's latest effort to win re-election or that double homicide at a local gin mill. Reporters don't have the boundless license to gleefully lie with words that fiction writers possess.

Sandburg's poetry is, in my opinion, some of the finest verse ever written by an American. But his nonfiction is perhaps even more notable. His biography of Abraham Lincoln is that rare commingling of authoritative historical writing and the lyrical use of the language of the poet, creating a unique and wondrous literary masterpiece.

Here, Sandburg describes Lincoln's final resting place:

Evergreen carpeted the stone floor of the vault. On the coffin set in a receptacle of black walnut they arranged flowers carefully and precisely, they poured flowers as symbols, they lavished heaps of fresh flowers as though there could never be enough to tell either their hearts or his.

And the night came with great quiet.

And there was rest.

The prairie years, the war years, were over.

Here, in the hands of a master, nonfiction reads like poetry. Note the specific attention to detail: "evergreen," "stone floor," "black walnut." The imagistic use of language: "they poured flowers as symbols." The poet's brevity: "And there was rest."

Define your subject

And this brings us back around to that oh-so important rule for non-fiction writing: Define your subject. This may sound obvious, but it is something that beginning writers (and sometimes seasoned pros) often give short shrift to as they plan their projects.

Vagueness is your enemy. Vagueness is the enemy of efficient and targeted research and, by extension, it is the enemy of interesting and effective writing. And perhaps worst of all, vagueness is *boring*.

If you do not have a specific, well-thought-out topic in the front of your mind when you begin your research, you will find yourself wandering around aimlessly in the world of sources and information. You may think you're writing about the Civil War, but what you're really trying to write about is the role of black soldiers in the Civil War, or the creation of the Confederate Flag, or how battlefield injuries were treated during the conflict.

For example, during my first year of college, I took a poetry-writing course taught by a Nobel-nominated poet named Dick Allen. The course was rewarding and I learned a lot, but if I had to tell you the single most important thing I learned during the course, I'd have to say it was being taught one simple rule for effective writing: *Be specific.*

This rule has served writers well for eons and I personally have never found it to fail. The best prose and fiction writers use it all the time, as do the finest songwriters and lyricists. The beauty of this rule is that it can also be applied to your technique as well as to your actual linguistic construction.

When you're writing, don't say "Music was playing in the background." Say, "A Beatles song was playing in the background." Or better yet, say "'Raining in Baltimore'

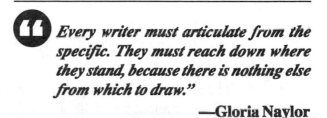

Every writer must articulate from the specific. They must reach down where they stand, because there is nothing else from which to draw."

—**Gloria Naylor**

by the Counting Crows was playing the background." (That example also illustrates the use of specificity in songwriting: The title is not "Raining in the City," it's "Raining in Baltimore.")

Examples abound throughout literature, historical biography, and non-fiction writing, as well as popular culture. Take the incredibly popular country/rock crossover star Shania Twain as an example. Her blockbuster *Come On Over* album contains some of the finest pop songwriting of today. A great part of the appeal of her songs is the specificity of her lyrics. In her song "When" (which is Shania's favorite on the album) she sings, "I'd love to...hear on CNN that Elvis lives again and that John's back with The Beatles...." In "That Don't Impress me Much," she sings to a suitor, "Okay, so you're Brad Pitt" and tells him "that don't impress me much." In "I'm Holdin' On To Love" she sings that "not even Dr. Ruth is gonna tell me how I feel...." The use of proper names of people, cities, groups, and so forth adds an aura of veracity to the writing that vague generalizations can't begin to achieve.

Therefore, you must deliberate on the narrowing of your subject until you know exactly what you're writing about and precisely what you're looking for. Ultimately, when the research process is over, you need to know what you want to say about the subject.

Zooming in

Here is an extensive list of some specific story examples to illustrate how the first step of effective research is moving from the general to the specific.

(And here is a hint before I move on. When in search of your idea, pretend you are being exposed to the material for the first time as a reader, *not* as the person who wrote it. This is difficult, yet it can save you a lot of time and grief if you keep your idealized reader in mind at all times. Let's face it: All the endless talk of writing for yourself aside, we do write to be *read*, right? Write.)

- Don't begin a project thinking you are writing about Amazon.com. Instead, write about how authors feel about Amazon's policy of publishing unedited customer book reviews.
- Don't begin a project thinking you are writing about American literature. Instead, write about the writing habits of five great American novelists.
- Don't begin a project thinking you are writing about Bill Clinton. Instead, write about Chelsea Clinton and the price the children of presidents pay growing up in the White House.
- Don't begin a project thinking you are writing about California. Instead, write about people who live in areas that scientists essentially guarantee will get hit by an earthquake…and then try to explain why they stay.
- Don't begin a project thinking you are writing about cancer. Instead, write about men who get breast cancer.
- Don't begin a project thinking you are writing about cats. Instead, write about why people who don't like cats think they're snooty, and people who love cats think they're the most magnificent creatures ever to walk on four legs.
- Don't begin a project thinking you are writing about football. Instead, write about all of the Super Bowl half-time shows of the past 10 years.
- Don't begin a project thinking you are writing about golf. Instead, write about the perfect hole in one.

- Don't begin a project thinking you are writing about Harvard. Instead, write about Harvard students who conduct Internet businesses from their dorm rooms.
- Don't begin a project thinking you are writing about health care in the United States. Instead, write about why a single aspirin costs $8 in an American hospital.
- Don't begin a project thinking you are writing about high blood pressure. Instead, write about the connection between people who have sleep apnea and its increased risk of high blood pressure.
- Don't begin a project thinking you are writing about Japanese food. Instead, write about the food safety concerns in preparing sushi.

> *Any writer who has difficulty in writing is probably not onto his true subject, but wasting time with false, petty goals; as soon as you connect with your true subject you will write."*
>
> **—Joyce Carol Oates**

- Don't begin a project thinking you are writing about Las Vegas. Instead, write about how casinos catch cheaters.
- Don't begin a project thinking you are writing about marriage. Instead, write about couples who fight constantly and yet refuse to split up.
- Don't begin a project thinking you are writing about music. Instead, write about rap. Or better yet, Christian rap.
- Don't begin a project thinking you are writing about Nazis. Instead, write about Hitler's health problems.
- Don't begin a project thinking you are writing about racism. Instead, write about a small town like Coeur D'Alene, Idaho, that loathes the fact that white supremacist groups have established base camps there and that the town is becoming known nationally for this.
- Don't begin a project thinking you are writing about shipping companies. Instead, write about one single package and track its entire journey.

- Don't begin a project thinking you are writing about Stephen King. Instead, write about the growing respect for King's work among scholars and academics, and his new status as an American literary icon.

- Don't begin a project thinking you are writing about The Beatles Instead, write about how John's relationship with Yoko may or may not have contributed to the break-up of the band.

- Don't begin a project thinking you are writing about the Catholic Church. Instead, write about Catholic priests' vow of chastity and how they manage to honor it (or not).

- Don't begin a project thinking you are writing about the Internet. Instead, write about pornographic Web sites that publish digitally altered photos of celebrities in compromising positions and how the rich and famous are responding to these supposed Fair Use "parodies" of their images.

- Don't begin a project thinking you are writing about the Kennedys. Instead, write about how John F. Kennedy Jr. died when a plane he was piloting crashed into the Atlantic.

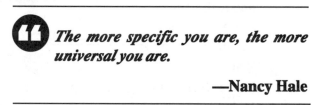

The more specific you are, the more universal you are.

—Nancy Hale

- Don't begin a project thinking you are writing about the legal system. Instead, write about why people hate lawyers.

- Don't begin a project thinking you are writing about the State of the Union address. Instead, write about the one member of the President's cabinet who is forbidden from attending the speech in case a bomb goes off in the building, wiping out the entire Presidential chain of succession!

- Don't begin a project thinking you are writing about the United States' economy. Instead, write about TV shopping networks that sell jewelry and the impact they have on the independent jeweler.

- Don't begin a project thinking you are writing about the weather. Instead, write about the worst blizzards in American history, the worst tornadoes in world history, or the worst earthquakes in North America.

- Don't begin a project thinking you are writing about UFOs. Instead, write about Roswell, N. Mex.
- Don't begin a project thinking you are writing about vitamins. Instead, write about the difference between beneficial megadoses and toxic levels of vitamins.
- Don't begin a project thinking you are writing about your mother. Instead, write about the day your mother gave you a check for your first year of college, money she had earned by working a second job for years and saving every penny of her wages…without telling you.

•••

Get the point?

Do you have your topic in mind? Good! Now it's time to immerse yourself in information…in step number one in my system: Immersion.

5 chapter

Step 1: Immersion

 *Acquire new knowledge while thinking over the old, and you may become a teacher of others.*

—Confucius

According to Webster's Dictionary, one of the definitions of the word "immersion" is, "baptism by complete submersion of the person in water." And the word "baptism" (once again according to Webster's Dictonary), has a specific non-religious meaning: "An act, experience, or ordeal by which one is purified, sanctified, initiated, or named."

These definitions, as you'll see, ring true when applied to the step of immersion in my research process.

So please make sure your seat back is in the upright position and that your safety belt is fastened. We are clear for takeoff. Onward!

When faced with a writing project that will undoubtedly require intensive research, I have found that the most effective first step for me is to immerse myself in data.

Immersion involves plunging head-first into your subject, to the point of being overwhelmed by information. But data immersion is not information overload for the sake of information overload.

The research process is a fascinating process, but it is actually more of a quest for insight. As a writer, one of the first things you need to do is to become thoroughly acquainted with the subject you want to write about.

At first, your research results and findings may seem to be too confusing. You may be looking at too much information, too soon. However, as you slowly work your way through the treasure trove of sources and resources available to you, an awareness of your subject will begin to permeate your consciousness. This awareness occurs at almost a subconscious level, but it does take place. As you repeatedly hunt down and review Web site descriptions, book titles, and magazine articles, you will begin to notice:

- Web sites that keep popping up no matter what search engine you use.
- Books that are repeatedly referred to.
- Authors' names that keep appearing in bibliographies.
- Articles and interviews that are constantly cited.
- Certain organizations are mentioned all of the time.

These are all clues that will help you assimilate the vast amount of data you will come upon and narrow down your sources to the key sites, authors, and other authorities that will be of the most use to you.

I have often had this happen during this first stage of my own research. Certain people, groups, universities, journals, magazines, etc. often rise to the top of the list of information sources when you begin hunting up material for a project.

A perfect example of this is my own body of work about Stephen King. I have been writing about Stephen King since the late 1980s. Anyone beginning a writing project about Stephen King and his work will come across my name repeatedly during his or her research. The wise writer will take this as a signal to check out my books if he or she wants to be adequately informed about Stephen King. There are a few other authors also very well-known for their work on King, and researchers will come across their names and would need to look into their books as well.

Admittedly, there is a danger with this approach—acquiring too much research material for your purposes—and drowning in a sea of information. For every one of my nonfiction books, without fail, I have always accumulated more articles, books, print-outs, interviews, photos, magazines, videotapes, and audio tapes than I end up using (or, in fact, that I could ever possibly use).

But the irony is that you really won't know if you can use something until you know if you can use it. Huh? Well, I'll explain:

When writing my book *The USA Book of Lists*, I bought two books I thought I would make good use of, *Sex Lives of the Presidents* by Nigel Cawthorne, and *Capital Confidential* by Bill Thomas. My thinking was to do several lists compiled from information gleaned from these books, including lists like "Presidential Mistresses," "White House Scandals," "Facts About Monica Lewinsky," "Politicians Who Have Abused Drugs and Alcohol," and other salacious (but undeniably fun to read) lists and features. These facts were already public knowledge and I thought it would add a steamy flavor to the book.

But as I worked on the book, I found myself gravitating toward facts about America that made me proud—not the stuff that embarrassed me. I found myself more interested in information like great things said by our Presidents, influential American achievements, and facts about the 50 states. The politicians' mistresses, details about their breast implants (the mistresses', that is), and politicians' notorious, behind-closed-doors shenanigans took second place in my search.

Throughout the writing of a book or magazine article, it is quite common for an author to bounce some ideas off editors to elicit opinions about material the writer is thinking about including in the project. This is universal to all publishers and it is a critical part of the complete publishing paradigm.

So I did what I always do when I have some doubts about tone, or approach, or appropriateness: I had a meeting with my editor. I asked what he thought about including raunchy stuff in the book.

Editors (the good ones anyway) will often ask an absolutely perfect question. The single question that will illuminate the issue with pinpoint clarity and allow the writer to make the decision about the material with added insight and a better grasp of the *publisher's* vision of the book.

If you are lucky, your editor (book or magazine) will also be a writer (as many of my editors are and have been) and will bring to the discussion an insight achieved only through having been through the same process you are now going through. Like they say in Hollywood, some of the best directors are the ones who started out as actors.

Regarding my *USA Book of Lists* query, my editor's question was, "If you include those kinds of lists in the book, do you think the White House Gift Shop or the Smithsonian Institution Bookstore will want to carry the book?"

Instantly, I knew the answer to this question was an unqualified no. The dubious lists were killed.

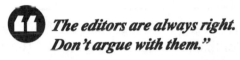

The editors are always right. Don't argue with them."

—Mark Skousen

There's an adage in the publishing industry that a book is the author's until he or she turns it in—then it belongs to the publisher. It is wise to prepare for the inevitability of your work being rejected, critiqued, or changed beyond recognition by keeping the lines of communication between writer and publisher open at all times.

I know that you're an artist, but there's a classic moment in the opening monologue of Woody Allen's best film of all time, *Manhattan*, that perfectly crystallizes the art/commerce convergence. Woody's character, writer Isaac Davis, is dictating the opening passage of a piece he's trying to write about New York. He describes the town as a place that "existed in black and white and pulsated to the great tunes of George Gershwin"; a town that he saw as a "a metaphor for the decay of contemporary culture," but which he still adored. As he continues

The best advice I've ever received was from my first editor, Paul C. Smith, as I began my column in July 1938: 'For God's sake, kid, be entertaining. And remember, I have a short attention span.'"

—Herb Caen

to expound on the negative aspects of New York, he suddenly stops and reminds himself not to get too heavy because, "Hey, we wanna sell some books here." (That phrase should hang above the desk of every writer who hopes to have some commercial success someday.)

Writers should never forget that is the ultimate goal. To borrow another morsel of Hollywood wisdom, the goal of publishing is to "put butts in the seats." (Hopefully, with your book.)

And the best way to achieve that is to make your writing as powerful, clear, and entertaining as possible.

The Internet

You will begin, or indeed you *must* begin, with an Internet search. If you're not online at home, you should be. But for those of you without computers, offsite Internet research can be done at your local public library, or your university library if you're an alum. (By law, university libraries that are U.S. Government Document Repositories are open to the public, regardless of whether you've ever attended the school or not.) Almost all libraries are connected to the Internet these days and they all allow free access. You may have to reserve your time in one-hour blocks and wait around if it's not your turn, but any time in a library can be put to good use, so don't fret if you're not allowed at the computer as soon as you walk in the door.

> *Computers are the most important thing to happen while I was growing up. I can get information a lot quicker than, say, going to the library.*
> **—Paul Sutusky, 17**

One huge difference between accessing the Internet from home and at the library is that at home you can download search results and documents onto your hard drive and peruse them at your leisure. With a click, you can "own" the materials you think might be useful.

While you're at the library...

At the library, you will more than likely have to print out the documents you will need to research more thoroughly. There may or may not be a per-page charge for printing using the library's printer. For example, at one university library I frequent, they charge by the page for print-outs off of microfilm or microfiche, as well as for photocopies. However, print-outs off their computers (either from CDs or material from the Internet) are free. Go figure.

In any case, be prepared, bring money, and make sure some of it is change for the photocopier. (Librarians sometimes get peeved if they are asked to make change.) Some libraries have change machines, but what will you do if they are out of change or out of order?

During this phase of the process, you will also search Barnes & Noble's Web site, Amazon.com's Web site, and used book services' Web sites for a list of books in print that relate to your subject, as well as relevant books that are out of print but still available. You could search the enormous database *Books in Print* itself (now up to more than 3,000,000 titles) either online or at the library, but you might end up with more titles than you can possibly work your way through. The books that stores are actually offering for sale, along with the out-of-print books that are for sale comprise a more targeted and easier-to-access source database than a complete list of every book in print about your subject.

Following your cybersurf, you should then plunder the *Reader's Guide to Periodical Literature* at the aforementioned local library, looking at the years pertaining to your topic, making note of magazines and newspaper articles relevant to your topic. Then you have to request the microfilm or microfiche copies of the magazines and newspapers on your list, find the articles, and print them out to take home and read and highlight.

You should then also review *The New York Times* Index for articles related to your topic. Not all libraries own *The New York Times* Index; so this may not be feasible in your area. *The New York Times'* Web site features a search feature, but it does not search the entire *Times* archive. Nonetheless, if you can access *The New York Times* (the "newspaper of record," after all) you will undoubtedly find much useful data you can make good use of.

The Lexis-Nexis information service can also be extremely useful. If you are a university alum and your alma mater subscribes to Lexis-Nexis, you should make use of this service. Lexis-Nexis is a computerized searchable database that returns full-text newspaper articles, plus full-text articles from general-interest magazines, specialized journals, and other valuable sources. You may need to pay for this service, so be warned: It can get very expensive...but the information may be worth the price.

While at the library, you should go through the library's card catalog (which may or may not be computerized). Make note of circulating books in the library that might be useful, but also, more importantly, look for reference books at the library that could also be helpful. These will have to reviewed at the library because they do not circulate, but often they are loaded with valuable information. Biographical encyclopedias, general encyclopedias, topic-specific encyclopedias (music, literature, politics, whatever), as well as dictionaries and anthologies, are all gold mines of facts.

If you want to save time, talk to the reference librarian, a highly trained and skilled library sciences professional who can steer you right to the books you will need and can also suggest other valuable sources.

When I was beginning the research for my book *The Italian 100*, which was a ranking of the most influential Italians in world history, I started with the Internet and the *Reader's Guide* and the book sources, but I also met with the reference librarian at the university library I use. Because my research needs for this book were wide-ranging and covered a great many disciplines, I needed more than just general sources and my reference librarian came through for me in a big way.

She showed me encyclopedias of canonized Roman Catholic saints for my Thomas Aquinas and St. Francis research; biographical encyclopedias of scientists for my Galileo, Fermi, and other science research; art encyclopedias for the painters and sculptors on my list; and music encyclopedias for the composers in my book. She was an enormous help and time-saver.

Throughout all this, you will need to keep your eye out for pertinent information and articles that you will want to photocopy or print out. Again, you will need to ascertain which books are relevant to your topic and then review them. To access the books, you can either read through them at the library (if they have them) or, if you want to own them, buy them at the bookstore.

Summary of research targets

1. An exhaustive Internet search for Web sites, books, articles, organizations, and other resources accessible online.
2. A review of the *Reader's Guide to Periodical Literature* at your local public or university library, followed by a review of pertinent findings.
3. A search of *The New York Times* Index (if available).
4. A search of Lexis-Nexis (if available).
5. A review of the library's card catalog for relevant books in circulation.
6. A meeting with one of the library's reference librarians for referral to important and relevant reference works.
7. A bookstore trip (if necessary).

● ● ●

By now, you will probably have file folders filled with many print-outs from Web sites, photocopies of magazine and newspaper articles, books, magazines, clippings, and other materials related to your topic.

Such a mountain of material may appear daunting at this point. However, you will ultimately work your way through it, selecting and rejecting data until you find what you need to write your project and begin to understand what you want to say about your subject.

chapter

The Seven Questions

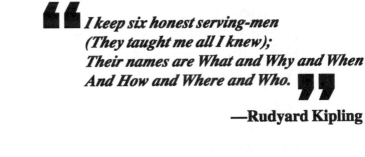

*I keep six honest serving-men
(They taught me all I knew);
Their names are What and Why and When
And How and Where and Who.*

—Rudyard Kipling

Before I continue with the six steps, I feel that it is important to mention the process you will need to use throughout your research. As a means of defining in your mind the true focus of your piece, you need to ask yourself seven very important questions. These seven questions are:

1. **Who?**
2. **What?**
3. **When?**
4. **Where?**
5. **Why?**
6. **How?**
7. **Weird?**

The first six of these questions are well known to journalism students and just about everyone in the communications industry. However, the seventh question (Weird?) is, I guess, my

own invention (or at least my own way of completing my individual research process).

Who?

Dry facts are like raw ingredients in a recipe: You need them to create your dish, but it takes a cook who knows what he or she is doing to put them together in a pleasing and palatable way. The people behind a story are the chefs who move the cooking process forward.

> *Personality is the supreme realization of the innate individuality of a particular living being. Personality is an act of the greatest courage in the face of life, the absolute affirmation of all that constitutes the individual, and the most successful adaptation to the universal conditions of existence coupled with the greatest possible freedom of personal decision."*
>
> **—Carl Jung**

The first question you should ask yourself as you begin your research is: Who is this about?

Even if you are writing about something as dry and potentially boring as Japanese monetary policy, you need to look behind the factual details and find the people in the story. Who are the men and women behind the decisions that affect Japanese monetary policy? What are they like?

Stories about boosts or drops in U.S. interest rates are a yawn and get placed in the money section of the newspaper. However, a story about who Fed chairman Alan Greenspan is dating gets a front page feature. Why? Because it is a natural human tendency to be interested in *people*, in the personalities involved, in the players who are causing the changes you are writing about, regardless of the topic.

Are you writing about dogs? Find a woman who adopts dogs every week and spends her money to take care of them until she can find them a home. Use her story as your lead.

Are you writing about vitamins? Find a man who lost all his hair from overdosing on vitamin A and use his story as a cautionary tale about megadoses.

Are you writing about the BeeGees? Find an interview with their mother and quote from it as a way of introducing each member of the group.

Are you writing about sports? Interview as many team doctors as you can get a hold of and sprinkle their comments throughout the piece.

Are you writing about trees? Interview an actual forest ranger as well as the plant manager of a paper manufacturing company.

Again, your first question should always be, *Who* is this about? And when you answer this question, as always, be specific.

What?

Your second question should be, "What is this about?" Don't fall back on the easy answer, which is the topic (or the title) of your work. There is always more than that to be determined. Good nonfiction reveals more than just the bare bones facts about a person's life.

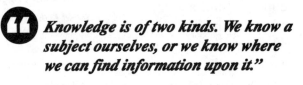

Knowledge is of two kinds. We know a subject ourselves, or we know where we can find information upon it."

—**Samuel Johnson**

Fiction can rarely compete with the high drama of reality.

During your immersion into your research, you will find yourself reading a great deal of what, at times, may seem like unrelated material.

But trust me on this: You never know when you will come upon a nugget of pure factual gold; something mentioned in passing by another writer, but which you can most definitely use to build an entire sequence around.

In addition to historical biography and the work of Stephen King (of which I am the world's authority, according to *Entertainment Weekly*), I also often write about popular culture and the entertainment industry. I have written about movies, TV shows, movie stars, and Hollywood. I am always reading magazines, watching E!, skimming through tabloids, reading celebrity biographies, and applying the Immersion technique of research as an ongoing effort.

I am always looking for new information and I am always looking for new book, novel, article, and screenplay ideas. And my experience has proven what I have said earlier: You *never* know when you will come upon a nugget of pure factual gold.

I subscribe to *Movieline* magazine and in a recent issue (April 2000) there was a feature titled "400 Hollywood Factoids." Any one of the items on this list could be an effective starting point for an article or even a book. However, some of them leaped off the page and shouted out at me to be researched and expanded.

Specifically, I found the following Hollywood factoids to be especially intriguing, any one of which could be the jumping-off point for an article, a speech, or a book—or they could just serve quite nicely as a conversation starter. As an exercise, we will look at a few of these potential story ideas.

Following the bulleted item, I offer a suggestion for the "big picture" project which these items could generate. (And these are all true, as unbelievable as some of they may seem.)

- Andy Garcia was born with a growth on his neck that was actually the remains of a twin brother or sister. (Stephen King used this premise for his novel, *The Dark Half.* A piece could be written about how common this is and what can be done about it.)

- Annabella Sciorra bathes four times a day. Woody Allen carries cans of tuna with him wherever he goes because he refuses to eat food that has been touched by someone else. Mike Myers has an aversion to being touched. Johnny Depp is terrified of clowns and collects insects. Kim Basinger is an on-and-off agoraphobic. Patty Duke is manic-depressive. Sean Penn keeps a mobile home permanently parked on the front lawn of his multimillion-dollar home in Malibu. Sting refuses to use deodorant. John Malkovich once ate nothing but Jell-O for 10 weeks. (Obsessive-compulsive behaviors and the neuroses of the rich and famous.)

- Anne Heche's father, who never admitted his homosexuality, died of AIDS at the age of 45. (Is homosexuality inherited?)

- Bill Paxton's father took him to see President Kennedy in Dallas the day JFK was assassinated. (Famous people who witnessed historical events.)
- Charlie Sheen has been known to tape his fingers together so he won't have to sign autographs. (Which celebrities willingly sign autographs and which do not? Why do fans consider autographs the ultimate celebrity collectible?)
- Daryl Hannah has chronic insomnia. (Famous insomniacs.)
- David Duchovny was a dissertation away from earning a Ph.D. in English literature at Yale when he quit school to become an actor. Matt Damon dropped out of Harvard at the end of his third year. Will Smith refused a scholarship to MIT in order to pursue his music career. (The meaning and value of an advanced degree, versus a person pursuing his or her true calling.)
- Demi Moore and Bruce Willis were married by Little Richard in a $500,000 ceremony on a sound stage. (How to become a legally ordained minister by mail.)
- Harrison Ford owns three airplanes and a helicopter. Nicolas Cage bought the Shah of Iran's Lamborghini. John Travolta owns a Boeing 707. Jay Leno owns more than 70 vintage cars and motorcycles. Aaron Spelling once had truckloads of imported snow dumped on the front lawn of his California home so his daughter Tori could experience a white Christmas. (Celebrity extravagances.)
- Jeanne Tripplehorn's father was a guitarist with Gary Lewis and the Playboys. Jon Voight's brother Chip Taylor wrote the songs "Wild Thing" and "Angel of the Morning." Treat Williams took his nickname from an ancestor on his mother's side, Robert Treat Payne, who was one of the signers of the Declaration of Independence. (Does "celebrity" run in families?)
- Jennifer Aniston is such an accomplished painter that one of her works was displayed at the Metropolitan Museum of Art when she was still in grammar school. Mira Sorvino speaks

fluent Mandarin Chinese. Edward Norton speaks fluent Japanese. (Actors who are also artists, musicians, sculptors, and writers—or who have other unexpected talents.)

- Mel Gibson and Geoffrey Rush were college roommates. Tommy Lee Jones and Al Gore were college roommates. Sharon Stone and Mimi Rogers were once roommates. Marlon Brando and Wally Cox were once roommates. Gene Hackman and Dustin Hoffman were once roommates. (Celebrity roommates.)

•••

There is a strange contradiction when you are doing effective research: Even though our goal is to focus, focus, focus, and be as specific as possible when writing and researching, we must also be sponges. ("General interest sponges," or "all-access sponges," you might call us.) We must always be on the lookout for new and interesting information that might turn into something we can write about. The secret is that the individual writer is the filter through which this information is passed. The end result is a particular vision, a specific perspective, a unique spin on the subject that no one but *you* can apply to a topic.

As an experiment, let's say your topic involves cats. Imagine how the following writers would interpret the subject of cats. (It doesn't matter whether it's fiction or nonfiction for the purposes of this exercise—the unique voice of each of these writers would dramatically surface in *either* format). These authors are: John Updike, Tom Wolfe, Stephen King, Saul Bellow, Tom Clancy, Joyce Carol Oates, Edna St. Vincent Millay, Ray Bradbury, Truman Capote, Sylvia Plath, John Cheever, F. Scott Fitzgerald, Thomas Pynchon, and Emily Dickinson.

These writers have such distinctive and memorable narrative voices that it was probably not too difficult to imagine the tone and style of the piece that any of these writers would have created if they had chosen to write about cats. (In fact, Stephen King already wrote a grisly short story titled "The Cat From Hell.") Each piece would be different even though the subject is about as mainstream and pedestrian as you can imagine.

When?

Defining the time period in which the events of your piece occur is just the beginning of answering the question of "when?"

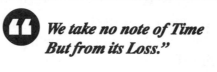

We take no note of Time But from its Loss."

—Edward Young

When doing your research you should be keeping your eyes open for interesting events that can be used to anchor your story and also add depth and texture.

A great deal can happen in only a decade. As part of the preliminary immersion research, we should peruse the history of that period and note important historical events, interesting developments, notable personalities, whatever. All of this can be used to spice up our narrative. After so much research, finding answers to "when?" can provide a fortuitous synchronicity, finding connections you didn't even think of.

So "when?" means more than just when something happened. It also means what went on during that period; information that often can be useful for the purposes of your piece.

Where?

There's an adage in the real estate business that says that there are only three important factors when it comes to selling a house, a building, or a piece of property: location, location, location.

We shall not cease from exploration And the end of all our exploring Will be to arrive where we started And know the place for the first time."

—T. S. Eliot

Redundancy aside, the adage is correct. A sense of place is critical to effective writing and can often be the element that elevates the piece from a simple narrative to something that captures the essence of a time, place, and series of events.

Read the next paragraph. Even though it is a work of fiction, note how the writer immediately places you exactly where he wants you to be: a small town in Ohio in the middle of summer. (And also note the incredible specificity, which adds enormously to the honesty and power of the passage.)

•••

Summer's here.

*Not **just** summer, either, not this year, but the apotheosis of summer, the avatar of summer, high green perfect central Ohio summer dead-smash in the middle of July, a white sun glaring out of that fabled Levi's sky, the sound of kids hollering back and forth through the Bear street Woods at the top of the hill, the **tink!** of Little League bats from the ballfield on the other side of the woods, the sound of power-mowers, the sound of muscle-cars out on Highway 19, the sound of Rollerblades on the cement sidewalks and smooth macadam of Poplar Street, the sound of radios — Cleveland Indians baseball (the rare day game) competing with Tina Turner belting out "Nutbush City Limits," the one that goes "twenty-five is the speed limit, motorcycles not allowed in it"—and surrounding everything like an auditory edging of lace, the soothing, silky hiss of lawn sprinklers.*

•••

This is the opening sequence of the novel *The Regulators* by Richard Bachman (a Stephen King pseudonym). Ask yourself this question: After reading this 155-word passage, do you know precisely *where* the story is taking place? I thought so.

So as part of your research, you need to read up on the environs of the place where your piece is set, the places your players travel through, and the locales that are critical to telling the story.

Effectively defining and describing *where* the events take place that you are recounting is the difference between two images you deliberately choose to insert into your reader's mind and consciousness. For example, here are two descriptions of the same room:

- "A room in a house."
- "A dark parlor with faded green orchid wallpaper, a dirty white divan with a tear on the right armrest, and a cast iron grating covered with dust, propped up in front of a fireplace that has not been used for 61 years."

Which image can you see more clearly?

Why?

The next question to ask is "Why?" "Why what?", you're probably asking yourself. The answer is, "Why did what happened, happen?" (Or, "Why did the events you are recounting in your work, happen?")

> *The improvement of understanding is for two ends: first, our own increase of knowledge; secondly, to enable us to deliver that knowledge to others."*
>
> **—John Locke**

Why did David Duchovny not simply write his dissertation and receive his Ph.D., even if he would never use it? Why do some celebrities loathe signing autographs? Why won't Sting use deodorant?

Admittedly, there is certainly no way of answering many of these questions. But simply posing the questions can allow you to speculate on the possible reasons behind a decision and in so doing, discuss larger issues.

Looking back at the story suggestions in "In the Beginning" on pages 32-35, there are a treasure trove of topics to consider for research. On looking at them, consider asking each one "Why?"

- Why does Amazon.com allow people to publish anything they want to say about any book Amazon sells?
- Why are so many writers alcoholics? (Or are they?)
- Why do people continue to live in earthquake-prone areas?

- Why are cats perceived as snooty and aloof?
- Why are there so many unwritten rules (don't mix styles, don't refuse to tour, don't wear sexy clothes) in the country music field?
- Why do men get breast cancer?
- Why does a single aspirin cost so much in an American hospital?
- Why do people like sushi?
- Why do people like rap?
- Why do healthy young males accept celibacy as a condition of becoming a Catholic priest? (Or do they?)
- Why do people hate lawyers? (Or do they?)
- Why do so many people take dangerous and deadly megadoses of vitamins?

As you immerse yourself in the research materials pertaining to your topic, you will find "Why?" questions presenting themselves to you. Some of these questions are going to be disposable, that is, they are either irrelevant, boring, or totally unnecessary to answer. But some of these queries are going to lead you into research that may provide fodder for important and entertaining insights for your piece.

"Why?" questions open the door to a fuller understanding of your topic, which, if acted upon and effectively utilized, will make for a book, article, speech, or term paper that says something new and fully engages your readers or listeners.

How?

You will find that pursuing the answer to the question of "why?" will often bring about the following question of "how?." There are usually layers of information surrounding a subject and we must first identify which particular "why?" we need to ask, a process that will lead us to understanding *how* events transpired.

Some examples...

- Asking why teen suicide is on the rise naturally leads to the question of how adolescents are killing themselves and what contribution this information might make towards understanding the problem.

- Asking why Japanese monetary policy is important to American fiscal policy naturally leads to trying to understand how the yen impacts the dollar and other global currencies.

> *Though I'd been taught at the dining room table about the solar system and knew the earth revolved around the sun, and our moon around us, I never found out the moon didn't come up in the west until I was a writer and Herschell Brickell, the literary critic, told me after I misplaced it in a story. He said valuable words to me about my new profession: "Always be sure you get your moon in the right part of the sky."*
>
> **—Eudora Welty**

- Asking why John Hinckley shot Ronald Reagan naturally leads to asking how he managed to get past the Secret Service and successfully shoot Reagan and two others.

- Asking why business and politics are becoming more and more intertwined these days naturally leads to discerning and examining specifically how corporations and the federal government are often working together toward common goals.

- Asking why the HBO series *The Sopranos* is so popular naturally leads to the question of how the writers have been able to so successfully portray Italian organized crime and how the members of the cast are able to so accurately capture the essence of the characters.

- Asking why so many writers have been alcoholics naturally leads to the question of how these talented artists are able to produce incredible literature while under the influence.

All of the "why" questions are subsets of the "how" questions and usually lead to further insights into the topic you are writing about.

When you come upon a piece of information that you suspect is important and that may be useful, ask yourself why it is important. Not only why did the events in question happen, but also why do you feel the information is important. This is a process that opens windows and doors into your mind.

Weird?

The question of "weird?" involves looking at your research materials and asking yourself what is weird about what you've found out. That is, you should look at your findings from an odd perspective; putting an offbeat spin on the facts, and seeing where it takes you.

This is the one question of the seven that is the most fun to answer. This is the question that asks you to look at your data through an odd looking glass and find the offbeat connections, the strange juxtapositions of information; and the just plain weird items that can add a great deal to your writing.

There really are no rules on how to find this stuff. It requires lots of reading and—for lack of a better term—daydreaming, especially of things you wouldn't automatically turn to as a source.

Remember my list of topic suggestions from Chapter 4? (If not, turn to page 32.)

While researching this topic, you would probably come upon nuggets of information that most definitely fit in the "weird?" category.

Here's something that I came across: Did you know that during President Bill Clinton's term as President, Chelsea Clinton's voice was rarely heard by the American people? Not on radio, not on TV, not in any public venue whatsoever. And even more fascinating is the fact that the decision for Chelsea to never speak publicly—under any circumstances—was a deliberate one on the part of her mother and father. This is weird information, and I could definitely use it.

And where did I find it? When I was engaging in my immersion, I was reading an issue of *USA Today* magazine (it's included in many

Sunday newspapers) and I came across a blurb about Chelsea's voice never having been heard in public. I did not know what I would ever use this for, or if I would even have the opportunity to use this fascinating factoid. However, I knew I had to "own" it, so to speak. So I made a note of this fact and, lo and behold,

> **"** *It's like making a movie: All sorts of accidental things will happen after you've set up the cameras. So you get lucky. Something will happen at the edge of the set and perhaps you start to go with that; you get some footage of that. You come into it accidentally. You set the story in motion, and as you're watching this thing begin, all these opportunities will show up."*
>
> **—Kurt Vonnegut**

it quickly came in handy for my book about American history, *The USA Book of Lists*. There is a chapter in that book called "The 130 Children of the Presidents of the United States" and I used it in an entry about Chelsea Clinton:

Chelsea Victoria Clinton (1980-)——Named for the Joni Mitchell song "Chelsea Morning"; Chelsea handled herself with dignity and grace during her father's scandal with Monica Lewinsky and following impeachment trial. In 1998, she entered college with thoughts of becoming an astronautical engineer or a doctor (or both?). From her father's inauguration until his retirement from the Presidency, Chelsea never spoke one word to the media or made one comment for the public record. Throughout her father's entire time in the White House, the American public didn't hear Chelsea Clinton speak.

The truth is that you never know when an interesting piece of information will be useful and come in handy. Prolific novelist J.N. Williamson once described writers as "noticers." Writers must always be paying attention.

Allow me to tell you the story of how my first book came into being. That experience was one of those moments of epiphany for me. Since that time, I have learned that you can actually choreograph your efforts so as to make these creative lightning strikes more likely. You cannot guarantee they will occur, of course, but you can help them along.

In 1983, I was re-reading J.R.R. Tolkien's *Lord of the Rings* trilogy for about the 600th time. (Well, perhaps not the *600th* time. Deliberate exaggeration is called *hyperbole* and is used for dramatic effect. Did it work?)

> **The most useful advice on writing I've ever received comes from Gil Rogin, who told me that he always uses his best thing in his lead, and his second best thing in his last paragraph; and from Dwight Macdonald, who wrote that the best advice he ever received was to put everything on the same subject in the same place. To these dictums I would add the advice to ask yourself repeatedly: what is this about?**
>
> **—Thomas Powers**

I had not yet sold my first book and I was still working full-time in our family jewelry business. I was browsing through a bookstore one day when I came upon a paperback by Robert Forster called *A Guide to Middle-Earth*. This book was an A to Z guide to the people, places, and things of Tolkien's *Lord of the Rings* trilogy. As I flipped through the book, I experienced the first of those moments I described earlier—an epiphany, a vision, a sudden instantaneous idea that presented itself to me with intense clarity. I immediately knew that I had come up with the idea for my first book, that it would sell, and that it would be successful.

That idea was an A to Z guide to the people, places, and things of Mayberry, North Carolina, as depicted on the TV series *The Andy Griffith Show*.

Applying a glossary format to a television series had never been done before and I instantly knew that not only *could* it be done, but that it would be welcomed with open arms by fans and be so well-received that it would be a groundbreaking book. And I was right.

The idea of taking popular culture seriously enough to use a pseudoacademic approach (using an encyclopedic dictionary format) to chronicle the specifics of a TV show is now commonplace. But my book

Mayberry, My Home Town was one of the first of its kind. It was a seminal moment in the cultural crossover between serious academic research and popular culture. Now, popular culture is taught in colleges and everything—from *Star Trek* to soap operas— is deconstructed and analyzed for themes,

> **You can't tell or show everything within the compass of a book. If you try to tell or show everything, your reader will die of boredom before the end of the first page. You must, therefore, ask yourself what is the core of the matter you wish to communicate to your reader? Having decided on the core of the matter, all that you tell him must relate to it and illustrate it more and more vividly."**
>
> **—Morris L. West**

significance, and influence. However, back in the mid-1980s, sitcoms were considered trivial and unimportant, even though many of the best were brilliantly written and superbly acted and produced.

Fifteen years ago I said that there was nothing trivial about Mayberry trivia and it still holds true today, but at an even greater intensity. *Mayberry, My Home Town* came out in hardcover in 1987 and the paperback is still in print today.

That moment in the bookstore is still vivid in my memory. I actually saw in my mind, in an instant, my completed book. I immediately knew that all I had to then do was research and write the thing...put the words on paper. The concept was that clear to me and it was all because I was just browsing through a bookstore with no intention of conceptualizing a book project.

What does the *Lord of the Rings* have to do with *The Andy Griffith Show*?

Nothing.

But thanks to the *Lord of the Rings*, the idea for my first book was given to me, like a gift. It was one of those moments of synchronicity that came about because I was not looking for it to come about.

So, to sum up, weirdness abounds in this world of ours, and it's just a matter of keeping our writer's antennae tuned to notice it. We must always be paying attention.

And then, once you find a factoid or a quote or an historical event that is unusual, ironic, or unexpected, the smart thing to do is to play with this item and see where it takes you. And these nuggets of information do not have to be *bizarre*—the literal definition of "weird" is not what we are looking for. "Slightly off-of-center" may be more accurate, perhaps. Weird tidbits open up new windows in the house of story you are building—whether it's a nonfiction house or a fiction house.

It should be noted that irony is always a powerful element for expanding a narrative, so pay special attention to those ironic moments that pertain to your subject when you come upon them in your research.

Let's say you are writing about the fifth anniversary of the Oklahoma City bombing. During your research you learn that there is one tree left standing on the site of the former federal building—it is the only living thing remaining there. It is a tree that withstood the full effects of the blast...and lived. This is a powerful image. It serves as an ironic metaphor for the theme of survival in the face of disaster. It shows nature defying the terrorists in the most dramatic way it can: by surviving.

That tree is nature contemptuously defying the psychotics who blew up the building and killed 168 people. (The story of this tree is true, by the way.) With eloquent silence, Mother Nature speaks loudly for the glory of life and negates the malevolent message the terrorists hoped would permeate American society by their actions.

These are evocative and poignant images, as well as being elements of a story that, if written from the heart, can speak volumes to anyone who reads it.

And that, in its essence, is your job. Now start asking questions.

Step 2: Notes

> **In 16th-century Europe it became much easier to make a creative contribution not necessarily because more creative individuals were born than in previous centuries or because social supports became more favorable, but because information became more widely accessible and easier to add to.**
>
> —**Mihaly Csikszentmihalyi**

The second step of my research process is essentially the preliminary note-taking process. The notes step begins when you begin putting down random thoughts, phrases, questions, images, facts, details, and other ideas related to your subject on paper. These notes will act as the foundation for your project. These note topics will have occurred to you as you read through the books, magazine articles, Web site documents, and other research materials you acquired during your initial immersion into your subject. I always save my notes. (And I don't mean until the article or the book comes out. I mean *forever*.)

To help you find all the information you'll need, ask yourself the seven questions. These questions will prove to be very effective tools in gathering your information.

Some writers I know dictate their notes at this stage of their project and then have them transcribed for review and modification later. To me, this seems to be double the work. Other writers type everything into their computers and avoid as much as possible ever writing anything by hand. Specific work habits are a personal choice and I do not recommend one type over another. Whichever system results in you compiling the info you need as efficiently as possible is the right system for you.

For me, it's pencil and legal pads. I need to see the words and the notes on paper laid out before me in order to conceptualize my approach to the material. I usually prefer pencil—specifically, a 0.7 mm, No. 2 mechanical pencil. The thicker 0.7 mm lead lends itself quite well to a firm hand and heavier pressure. When I am in a flurry of note-taking, I tend to break the leads on the thinner pencils.

Some writers dictate their notes and are very comfortable with completely *verbalizing* their thoughts and notes, feeling no need whatsoever to actually *see* their

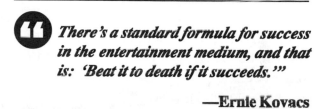

There's a standard formula for success in the entertainment medium, and that is: 'Beat it to death if it succeeds.'"

—Ernie Kovacs

ideas on paper. Fine. Writing is a sensory act and it's a personal decision as to which senses you wish to use. If speaking and hearing your notes works for you, and you are serious about writing regularly and publishing when you can, then just make sure you've always got lots of blank tape and plenty of spare batteries on hand at all time.

I wrote down many notes for my 1998 book, *The Complete Titanic.* This was a project offered to me during the peak of the Titanic mania that followed on the heels of the release of the 1997 James Cameron weeper, *Titanic.*

Writers who have done several books for a publisher will sometimes be offered projects. It's a little-known fact that many publishers have a "Books Looking for Authors" list. This is a list of ideas generated in-house by the company's editorial team, often working in conjunction with the marketing department. It is quite common for a writer who has worked with a publisher to be offered the opportunity to write books from this list.

That was the case with my book about the Titanic. My publishers at the time, Carol Publishing Group, decided they wanted a book about the Titanic to be part of their catalog. The nature of the subject convinced them that the book would remain a part of their backlist as well.

The editorial board involved in conceptualizing the Titanic book knew what they did *not* want: another slapped-together mish-mosh of ubiquitous material rehashing the Titanic story. Nor did they want a book about the movie directed by James Cameron. Sure, the movie could be covered in a book about the Titanic, but my publisher was looking for something with some historical weight to it; a book that would have some resonance and longevity.

When I pursued the list of published volumes about the Titanic, I realized that coming up with a new approach to the subject was not an easy task. The sinking of the Titanic is believed to be one of the three subjects that have been (and continue to be) written about the most in the English language. The Civil War and Christ are alleged to be the other two.

Admittedly, it was a daunting task, but I did my homework. Even though I turned a few corners into dead ends, I *Good order is the foundation of all good things."*

—Edmund Burke

believe my final result—*The Complete Titanic: From the Ship's Earliest Blueprints to the Epic Film*—is a fresh approach to the Titanic's history and legacy.

The following list is one of the final versions of the original master note list I compiled when I began researching my book. (I transcribed these items instead of scanning in my original handwritten notes. I wanted to spare you having to endure and decipher my scribblings—it's not a pretty sight.)

- Title idea: The Ultimate Titanic Book of Knowledge? (no)
- better title?
- the sinking
- what the 1,500 felt
- the people
- Harland & Wolff
- read novels (Danielle Steel!!)
- read books & take notes

- the journey
- the movie
- complete cast? only majors? interviews? can I get to Cameron? Winslet? is there time?
- Interviews—from pre-launch through movie?
- Carpathia
- the passengers
- crew
- A to Z?
- Lifeboats
- Who's Who?
- salvage expeditions
- Ballard—try and get interview?
- survivors
- Titanic Historical Society—join
- other Titanic groups worth talking to?
- list of recovered artifacts? complete? partial? photos?
- bibliography
- reprints of public domain articles
- Captain Smith—his profound embarrassment
- Smith's last words
- Harold Bride—important—NY Times piece
- Titanic owned by J. P. Morgan
- Ismay; traditionally the bad guy—justified? Do point/ counterpoint-type essay?
- White Star? Any interest here?
- facts and figures
- the musical
- speed
- telegrams—reproduce in their entirety? (yes)
- guns on Titanic?
- did Murdoch commit suicide?—pros/cons

- stats—length, weight, etc.—separate section?
- official registry documents?
- newsgroup postings? anything there?
- computer games?
- Florida Museum?
- "Everything There Is To Know About the Titanic"?? (yuk!)
- media coverage through the years
- food—complete list (yes)
- cargo—complete list? (yes)
- Wreck of the Titan—public domain—reprint (enough space? 35,000 words?)
- A Night to Remember
- myths and rumors
- maps?
- 60,000 words?
- 75,000 words? more?
- Californian—Pro-Lordites/anti-Lordites
- Scientific American articles? (yes)
- "Fascinating Facts" feature? (boring!)
- "Nearer My God To Thee"
- brittle metal
- section titles—Immortal Titanic Saga—Mysteries of the Titanic Legend—etc.
- Engineering News—reprint?
- Lightoller
- International Marine Engineering
- oceanliner.com—catalog of ocean liner stuff
- alt.history.ocean-liners.titanic
- Olympic class liners—largest vessels ever built at their time
- "Autumn"
- Band not insured
- Complete repertoire of band? (yes)

- A&E documentary
- Gilded Age
- Ken Marschall
- Dan Butler (e-mail him)
- Eaton & Haas
- Don Lynch—has cameo in movie
- Titanic Live—NBC—Sarah James
- eBay—list of Titanic items?—no
- "Her name has evolved into a metaphor for many things since April of 1912."

•••

This original list of items was picked apart, reconsidered, rearranged, expanded, loathed, loved, dissected, endlessly reviewed, and ultimately shaped into what is now the table of contents of my book. (My final *Complete Titanic* table of contents is reproduced in its entirety in Chapter 9.)

You can see that each of these bulleted points is a relevant area of information that needs to be explored (or immediately ruled out). Having this master list of shorthand note topics provided me with a blueprint for my researching. In fact, if your general notes list is specific enough, you can work your way through the items, researching each topic one by one, and then checking off each item after you have determined what is important and what can be (and must be) disregarded.

This kind of stream-of-consciousness brainstorming on paper is invaluable and absolutely necessary for your project to begin to take shape.

Even though it doesn't seem possible during the early stages of researching a project, your writer's mind will miraculously transform a wide range of confusing and disparate materials into an accessible organization of meticulously refined facts.

chapter

Step 3: Review and Think

his is the step in which you review your selectively culled compilation of notes, go through every item on your list one by one, and make a decision as to whether or not this note topic is something worth pursuing and including in your work.

For my book, *The Complete Titanic*, I rejected many items as either uninteresting, irrelevant, or too much work to learn about compared to the resultant benefit to the reader.

Here are some useful criteria for determining what to include and what to leave out as you go through your list of notes:

- Is this critical information necessary to making my project as comprehensive as possible?
- Will I be able to track down the information I need efficiently and in a thorough enough manner so that I will be able to write confidently about this topic?
- Is this topic interesting?

- Is this topic so broad that it would be a waste of time to try and tackle it within the parameters of my project?
- Does this topic really belong in this project?
- Is there a chance I can find new, intriguing information about this topic that will make my project extremely valuable and of high academic merit?
- Even if I want to cover a certain marginal topic, will I have time to include it? If I prioritize my time and my allotted word count, is this topic important enough to include?
- Am I personally interested in researching this specific topic?
- Can a marginal topic be utilized as a sidebar or an appendix by the inclusion of an exclusive interview or some reprint material?
- Will my coverage of this specific topic survive legal scrutiny (in the case of a book or magazine article)?
- Will covering this topic require photos or text reprint material, for which I will have to pay a fee? If so, can I afford the costs?

If you apply these questions to your master list of notes, you should be able to pick and choose appropriately, with the ultimate result being your working table of contents.

To help clarify things for you, take these words of Jacob Rabinow, famous inventor, to heart:

> *You must have the ability to get rid of the trash which you think of. You cannot think only of good ideas, or write only good music. You must think of a lot of music, a lot of ideas, a lot of poetry, a lot of whatever. And if you're good, you must be able to throw out the junk immediately without even saying it. In other words, you get many ideas appearing and you discard them because you're well trained and you say, "that's junk." And when you see the good one, you say, "Oops, this sounds interesting. Let me pursue that a little further." And you start developing it. Now, people don't like this explanation. They say, "What? You think of junk?" I say, "Yup. You must." You cannot a priori think only of good ideas. You cannot think only of great symphonies. Some people do it very rapidly. And this is a matter of training.*

chapter

Step 4:
Table of Contents

 Be regular and orderly like a bourgeois, so that you may be violent and original in your work.

—**Gustave Flaubert**

The term "table of contents" usually refers to the contents of a book. But I have always found it extremely useful to use the table of contents paradigm for more than just my books. Traditionally, a table of contents is a feature found *only* in books or magazines. Yet, I have compiled what can justifiably and accurately be described as a table of contents for everything from articles, interviews, and essays, to letters and speeches. I have always found the technique to be a good way of visualizing a clear, logical, chronological outline of the material I will be covering in the piece I am writing.

Unlike the notes step of this process, the table of contents is specific. The notes step of our research process is where you:

- Annotate your bulleted points.
- Move things around.
- Ask yourself questions in the margins.
- Asterisk certain sections for later review.

- Add additional relevant notes at the bottom of the page, not worrying one whit about topic headers, sub-headers, sidebars, whatever.

The Notes section, as we discussed earlier, is more stream-of-consciousness and is "all over the map," so to speak.

The working table of contents, on the other hand, is tight and structured, and the logical follow-up to the Review and Think step of my system. Your working table of contents should be detailed but not meandering.

The term "table of contents" can describe the working outline for your piece, as well as the final published contents of a book. Your table of contents is the blueprint of a coherent and logical work, laid out in a rational order, that accurately covers your subject.

By forcing yourself to write a working table of contents immediately after the Review and Think selection process, you are able to move headings and complete sections around, rearrange features, delete items, and manipulate the individual components of the book easily and quickly. Plus, you always have—at a glance—a one- or two-page blueprint of your book, which you will find to be extremely useful in keeping you focused.

Remember my list of scribblings about the Titanic from the Notes section? That list comprised my rough compilation of facts, ideas, questions, suggestions, and other elements of the Titanic saga, all of which I uncovered during my Immersion and reading phase.

That compilation of random data was eventually transformed into the table of contents for the final book. To illustrate this thematic metamorphosis, I reproduce here the final table of contents, as published in *The Complete Titanic*.

If you compare my list of notes with this final table of contents, you will see some things used as originally noted, some items deleted, some things moved around, and some features reworked and revised into something quite different from what I originally jotted down.

I'm sure you've heard writers refer to a piece that "wrote itself." That actually happens. It is a wondrous experience to have done the research and become so well-versed in your subject that an enormous pile of writings and ideas begins to rearrange itself in your mind, almost at a subconscious level, until the work begins to write itself!

The Complete Titanic

From the Ship's Earliest Blueprints to the Epic Film

by

Stephen J. Spignesi

Contents

The Text of the Titanic "Death Message"
Sent by the R.M.S. Olympic on April 15, 1912

R.M.S. Titanic: Doomed Ship of Dreams

I. The Titanic Files:
A Complete Chronicle of the Titanic Disaster

1. Titanic on the Record

- Titanic's Original "Transcript of Register," March 25, 1912
- Titanic's Original "Certificate for Clearance," April 11, 1912
- Titanic's Original "Survey of Emigrant Ship," April 12, 1912

2. The Titanic Timeline: A Year-by-Year, Day-by-Day, Minute-by-Minute Account of the Titanic Tragedy and the Aftermath, 1850 - 2002

3. Last Meals: Dining on the Titanic

- The Complete Titanic Foodstuffs Inventory
- The Complete Titanic Tableware and Linens Inventory

4. Calling for Help: The Complete Texts of the 70 Titanic Marconigrams, from the Collision with the Iceberg through the Carpathia Docking in New York

- The 36 Ships at Sea on the North Atlantic the Night Titanic Foundered
- Carpathia's Captain Rostron's Preparations for Receiving the Titanic Survivors

5. The Lifeboats: The Truth Will Never Be Known

- The Contents of the Titanic's Lifeboats After the Rescue

- The C. M. Lane Life Boat Co.'s Appraisal of the Gear
  Recovered from the Titanic's Lifeboats

6. A Titanic Who's Who
- The Complete Titanic Cargo List

7. In Their Own Words: Two Titanic Survivors Speak

8. Asking Questions: A Comprehensive Look at the British Commission of Enquiry's Report on the Loss of "Titanic"
- King George V and Queen Mary's Message of Sympathy to the
  Managing Director of the White Star Line and President William
  Howard Taft and President Taft's Telegram of Condolence to King
  George V

9. The Last Pilgrimage: The 28 Most Important Findings from the Final Report of the U.S. Senate Subcommittee Titanic Hearings
- The 86 Witnesses Who Testified at the U.S. Senate
  Subcommittee Hearing into the Titanic Disaster
- The U.S. Senate Subcommittee Testimony of Guglielmo
  Marconi
- The U.S. Senate Subcommittee Testimony of Californian
  Captain Stanley Lord
- Excerpts from J. Bruce Ismay's U.S. Senate Testimony
- J. Bruce Ismay's Official Statement to the British Media
  Following the U.S. Senate Hearings
- The U. S. Senate's Official Summary of Titanic Souls Lost and
  Saved

II. On Titanic: A Journal of Original 1912 Writings
10. The First *New York Times* Story About the Titanic Tragedy

11. Marconi Operator Harold Bride's First-Person Account

12. The Titanic Accounts of Dr. Washington Dodge and Mrs. Dodge

13. *The New York Evening Journal* April 16, 1912 Front Page Editorial

14. Two Articles from the April 1912 *Scientific American*

•••

You will notice that my book was compiled from many sources; it is essentially a varied combination of primary sources, secondary sources, original research, photos, drawings, Internet research, article reprints, and government documents.

Researching *The Complete Titanic* truly tested my ability to immerse myself in my research…and at times I worried that I would end up drowning. As I said before, it is inevitable that you will always end up with more material and information than you can possibly use.

But this is how it should be. After all, how can you know what kind of car you like unless you look at a million cars? How can you know what kind of house you like unless you look at a million houses? How can you know what to name your kid unless you consider a million names?

Do not be concerned about assembling *too much* information. The only thing you need to focus on is doing as much research as you can within the time frame you have allocated for research.

As you sift through the articles, books, interviews, videos, etc., always keeping the subject of your piece at the forefront of your writer's mind, the good stuff will sift through and you will ultimately use what you need to use to keep *your* vision of the piece true.

chapter

10

Step 5: Chapter by Chapter

> **Fear is the enemy of creativity. It clenches you up.**
>
> —**Lawrence Kasdan**

It's magic time. This step has a very straightforward mandate: Begin writing your work.

By this stage of the game, you have read through all your materials and made copious notes. You have reviewed these notes and refined them into a working table of contents. The magic will now take place as a joint effort of your conscious and subconscious minds working together to make the words flow.

Do not be afraid to start writing; be confident. You can always rewrite later. For now, get the words on paper (or on screen, as the case may be).

The Chapter by Chapter phase requires you to start at the beginning and write one chapter at a time (I'm using the word "chapter" figuratively, except in the case of a book, of course). You will carefully follow your table of contents until you have a complete first draft of your book, magazine article, speech, or term paper. For each chapter, you must ask yourself the seven questions and write your text to be relevant to your responses to those questions and to be a means of further developing the ultimate point you wish to make with your work.

This step of the Six Step process is simple and elegant. Yet, from an artistic standpoint, it is perhaps the most difficult. This is where you step up to the plate, where your bluff is called, where you sign on the dotted line.

This is where you have to turn it out.

This part of the process is all you. The earlier steps were you, too, of course, but they required mechanical, more clinical, more nuts-and-bolts type work.

I'll say it again: This part of the process is all about you. It is your voice that your readers, listeners, and professors want to hear.

When it comes to content, though, a caution: Do not try and write what you think they will want to hear. Instead, write what you want them to know, and do it one chapter at a time.

Keep an eye on your word count at all times, but do not lock yourself into an arbitrary count per chapter if you find yourself in the zone and that the words are flowing. You can always rearrange and revise later. For now, write with your target word count per chapter in mind, but allow yourself the freedom to wing it if so inspired.

And now, some examples...

The following eight examples represent fine nonfiction writing—expository writing that provides information, of course, but also does much more.

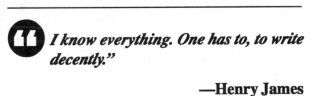

I know everything. One has to, to write decently."

—Henry James

This first excerpt is drawn from the chapter "Galactic Map" from the book *The Creation of Matter: The Universe from Beginning to End* by Harald Fritzsch (Basic Books, 1984). In this book, Fritzsch, a professor of physics at the University of Munich, presents serious scientific information for the general reader. However, he never loses sight of the profound awe the wonders of creation can instill in the observer.

•••

It was an unusually clear, moonless night. Above me was the great span of the Milky Way. The faint glow of the stars guided me through the summer night, lighting my way through the Hungarian landscape. My canoe glided quietly in the calm stream, with only an occasional correction by me to keep my little craft on course, and I was able to concentrate on the stars in the sky.

The Milky Way, the ribbon of stars stretching over the sky from north to south, is our galaxy, a system containing about a hundred billion stars, one of which is our sun—merely one of many stars at the rim of this disk-shaped galaxy. When we look at the ribbon of the Milky Way we are, in a manner of speaking, looking into the disk, that is, along the plane on which the galaxy is spread.

During my night journey through Hungary I could follow the slow progress of the ribbon across the sky—a consequence of the earth's rotation, like the sun's journey from east to west in daytime. I looked eastward, out of the galactic plane. Here the naked eye can make out stars in the vicinity of the sun, stars that are still part of our galaxy. But behind that there is nothing but intergalactic space.

•••

The second excerpt is from a fascinating book called *Deadly Doses: A Writer's Guide to Poisons* by Serita Deborah Stevens and Anne Klarner (Writer's Digest Books, 1990). This book teaches you how to poison people in a wide variety of ways (in your stories, of course). The authors even provide a series of appendices in which you pick and choose the symptom or symptoms you would like your character to experience and the authors tell you which poison will do the job most effectively (atropine, benzene, blue-ringed octopus, byrony, calcium, cobra, hemlock, jimsonweed, pavulon, and many more). The writers not only communicate the scientific facts about poisons of all kinds, but also teach readers how to make the most effective use of the information in their writing in an informative and entertaining way.

•••

Historically, arsenic was the murderer's most popular tool, primarily because it was found in so many common household items from wallpaper and paste to paints and pesticides. Nobody thought anything if you went into the pharmacy (chemists in Great Britain) to get rat poison. Of course, the Borgias and de Médicis had their own private supply.

•••

This third excerpt is from a truly unique volume called *The Story the Soldiers Wouldn't Tell: Sex in the Civil War*, by Dr. Thomas P. Lowry (Stackpole Books, 1994). The excerpt is from the chapter titled "I Take Pen in Hand...." It is an illustration of the research Lowry did for his book, as well as an excellent example of how to apply the "weird?" question to an area of historical lore that would seem to be "tapped out" in terms of new information. By focusing on the very specific area of sexual activities during the Civil War, Dr. Lowry has written a book that is not only important for its historical revelations, but which is also an entertaining and engaging read. After all, sex sells—besides, it's fun to read about.

•••

In the War Between the States, so many soldiers wrote letters that it contributed to a nationwide paper shortage. The mail carried millions of epistles. A substantial but lesser number of men and women kept diaries. Many of these have been published, but in the four generations since the war, the heirs, editors, and descendants of those writers and diarists have expurgated, purified, bowdlerized, amputated, and gelded the surviving material. Precious little has escaped the censor. But here and there enough has survived that we can reconstruct a history of the earthy side of the war, as a paleontologist may describe an extinct animal from a single bone.

•••

The fourth excerpt is from a lengthy article by Stephen King called "Head Down." It was originally published in *The New Yorker* magazine (April 16, 1990), and later collected in his book *Nightmares & Dreamscapes* (Viking, 1993). "Head Down" is about, of all things, the prosaic subject of Stephen King's son Owen's Little League baseball team. Yet, King writes the team's story in such a vivid and lively manner, that it ends up reading like one of his best short stories. "Head Down" is a fine example of how nonfiction can be as moving and interesting to read as the finest fiction.

•••

Nolan Ryan, probably the greatest fastball pitcher ever to play the game of baseball, likes to tell a story about a Babe Ruth League tournament game he pitched in. He hit the opposing team's leadoff batter in the arm, breaking it. He hit the second batter in the head, splitting the boy's helmet in two and knocking him out for a few moments. While this second boy was being attended to, the number three batter, ashen-faced and trembling, went up to his coach and begged the man not to make him hit. "And I didn't blame him," Ryan adds.

•••

The fifth excerpt is from a classic called *The Italians* by Luigi Barzini (Bantam, 1965). This book is described as "a full-length portrait featuring their manners and morals," but that blurb does not do this incredible book justice. *The Italians* looks at Italian culture, character, behavior, and more, but what the blurb does not reveal—but the excerpt does—is the lyrical, almost poetic use of language by Barzini. Barzini's masterpiece is a text-book example of how to elevate nonfiction narrative to the level of high literary art. The facts are there, but Barzini also captures the intangible with his writing—the heart, the soul, the essence of Italy and the Italians.

•••

There are sultry days in July and August when the cities, emptied by the natives, are almost completely taken over by the swarms of dusty and perspiring foreigners. During the siesta hour, when even the carriage horses sleep under their straw hats, the relentless tourists finally slow down. They bivouac everywhere. They recline on park benches, kerbstones, the stone brims of fountains, or ancient ruins. They place their heads over crossed

arms on cafe tables for a siesta among the empty bottles, the dirty nap-
kins, and the recently purchased souvenirs. They then really look like a
tired and bedraggled army after a fatiguing battle, who have occupied a
city abandoned by their fleeing enemy. They have conquered. The place is
theirs.

•••

The sixth excerpt is from the first and second editions of my book,
JFK Jr. (Carol Pub. Group, 1999). The first edition of my book, which
came out in early 1997, was titled *The JFK Jr. Scrapbook* (Carol Pub.
Group, 1997) and was complete through John's wedding in September
1996. I updated the book in the summer of 1999 after John died in a plane
crash and a second edition was published that fall. The excerpt includes
material from the first edition plus some of the new material I wrote for the
second edition. When writing my update, I kept in mind that nonfiction
does not need to be emotionless, but that the nonfiction writer must remain
objective.

In my 1999 update, I decided to present the facts as dispassionately
as possible, because the entire nation was in a state of mourning when the
second edition was published and I knew that my book would be around
long after the last tribute to John had been spoken. In this case, I felt that
simply chronicling the facts was enough. There is more of a nostalgic tone
in my earlier words about John. I did not want that for the new material
because the tears shed for John were already flowing when my updated
edition was published. Sometimes the gravity of a situation carries with it
such profound, universal emotion that the writer simply needs to report
the facts, and leave interpretation to history. Knowing how to fine-tune
your tone is one of the most difficult tasks for a nonfiction writer and that
is part of the magic we discussed earlier.

•••

Photogenesis: The life of John F. Kennedy Jr. has been like a quick-
silver succession of photographic images, all of which are indelibly etched
into the collective consciousness of America.

We all have seen the photo of John as a 2-year-old infant crawling around under the big wooden desk of his father, the president; and we have all also seen—countless times—3-year-old John saluting the coffin of his slain father. From there, the images blur into one long succession of pictures of John as a young boy, as a gangly teen (with a huge halo of curly hair), and into later views of John as the handsome young man one woman writer I know described as an Adonis.

America has watched John grow up; we've followed him through his school years, into college, on his travels, through law school, and, of course (much to John's chagrin), we've been along on many of his dates. And even though his political involvement has been extremely limited, there exists in this country a perception that we are simply biding our time, patiently waiting until John is ready to run for public office.

John is the hesitant heir to Camelot. The kingdom would seem to be his for the taking—if he ever decides he wants it.

(Fast forward two years...)

At 9:40 p.m., John's plane began to plunge towards the sea at a rate of almost a mile a minute—almost 10 times faster than a plane that size would normally descend. According to aviation experts, this kind of rapid descent indicated either that John's plane had experienced a major malfunction, or that John had become totally disoriented and a victim of what is known as "black hole vertigo"—an inability to distinguish up from down. John's plane hit the water.

After it was confirmed that John's plane was seriously overdue, a massive search and rescue operation began within hours. News reports electrified the world as people, hoping and praying for the safety of the three, waited by their radio and television sets for the latest word.

Debris from John's plane soon began washing up on the shore of Martha's Vineyard and on Sunday, July 18, authorities switched their operation from a "search and rescue" to "search and recover"—confirmation that officials believed there were no survivors of the crash. All hope had vanished.

•••

The seventh excerpt is from the chapter "Family Matters" from the book, *Robert Todd Lincoln: A Man in His Own Right* (University of

Oklahoma Press, 1969). This paragraph is a textbook example of fine nonfiction expository writing. It is specific, tightly written, relates an entertaining and interesting anecdote, and includes firsthand quotes by the people being written about.

•••

Of course there is evidence of an occasional disagreement within the Lincoln household involving father and son. The artist Carpenter, while staying at the White House in 1862, related that Robert burst into John Hay's room and exclaimed, "Well I have just had a great row with the President of the United States." This "row" involved Tad, who, as usual, had gotten away with something for which he should have been punished. What could be more natural than an older brother being frustrated because a doting parent would not correct a younger child? On the other hand, there are examples of Abraham Lincoln's fondness for his eldest son. Noah Brooks recalled that the president once, in referring to Tad's rearing, said, "Let him run, there's time enough yet for him to learn his letters and get poky. Bob was just such a little rascal, and now he is a very decent boy." It would seem best to conclude that between Abraham Lincoln and Robert T. Lincoln there existed a reasonably normal father and son relationship, and to attempt to prove the contrary is difficult if not impossible.

•••

The eighth and final excerpt is also about Lincoln's oldest son, Robert Todd, but this selection is from Ruth Painter Randall's masterful biography *Lincoln's Sons* (Little, Brown, 1955). You will notice that Randall writes her account of Mary Todd Lincoln's commitment trial like a scene from a novel. Again, the writer is very specific and uses direct quotes while presenting the dramatic facts. The result is gripping and powerful writing that stays with the reader long after the book has been closed.

•••

He was asked if he regarded it as safe to allow his mother to remain unrestrained. He answered, "She has long been a source of much anxiety to me," and again he was affected to tears. He said she had always been "exceedingly" kind to him. In his opinion she had been of "unsound mind" since the death of his father, had been "irresponsible" for the past ten years. She was "unmanageable" and would never heed his advice. He told of her purchases which had no reason, "for her trunks are filled with dresses and valuables of which she makes no use. She wears no jewelry and dresses in deep black."

The jury returned a verdict of insanity. Robert then went up to his mother and took her hand tenderly. She looked at him sadly and reproachfully and exclaimed, "O Robert, to think that my son would ever have done this." He turned his face away that she might not see the pain in it.

Should you rewrite your masterpiece?

You will write your project chapter by chapter. Chapter by chapter the words will pile up until the day comes when you write the last sentence of the last chapter. As you are writing these chapters, should you rewrite as you're writing, or wait until the whole thing is finished?

> *You don't write because you want to say something; you write because you've got something to say.*
>
> **—F. Scott Fitzgerald**

That is completely up to you. Personally, I reread my work every five or six paragraphs and make minor revisions on the spot. I also do my major "Review and Polish" (Step 6) revision, but I find it easier to make small tweaks as I go along.

Do whatever is right for you. Find the system that works best for you. But get those chapters written. You know their titles, you know how many words each chapter has to be, you have the information necessary to write them.

So just do it. And when you are finished, what you will have created will be the definitive expression of your vision of the subject, the result of becoming an instant expert on your topic, because you wrote down what you want people to know about what *you* learned.

chapter

Step 6:
Review and Polish

❝ *Trifles make perfection, and perfection is no trifle.* **❞**

—**Michelangelo**

s the Chapter by Chapter step is all about the *writer* in you, the Review and Polish step is all about the *reader* in you.

This final step of my six-step research and writing approach is an important one. Why? Because this is your last chance to get it right. And because getting it right involves a careful critique of your piece to find what's wrong with it, let us begin with a pronouncement: Rules for writing are dangerous.

Okay, I take it back. *Some* rules for writing are dangerous. After all, blanket statements and generalizations are frowned upon, aren't they? (I read that in a book of rules for writing.)

If all the nitpicky, arcane rules for writing are followed blindly, meaning, with a willingness to second-guess what you mean to say, instead of worrying about how you say it...well, if there's a better way to stifle creativity, I'd like to hear about it. However, don't throw away the rules...just be sure of your message and worry about the mechanics later.

One of the classic examples of this paradox (writing has rules; rules stifle creativity) is the strict application of the rule that tells us not to end a sentence with a preposition.

If this was mindlessly obeyed, it is possible that one of your fictional characters (if you write novels or short stories) would ask another, "From where are you?" instead of "Where are you from?" Of course, some grammatical rules are no-brainers and must be adhered to unless you want to come off as a simpering, illiterate idiot who shouldn't be allowed anywhere near a keyboard (or even pencil and paper, for that matter).

Many of these unbreakable rules were patiently itemized in William Safire's 1990 book *Fumblerules*. The most notable of these rules (and perhaps the most important as well) include making sure verbs agree with their subjects ("Verbs *has* to agree with their subject") and not using double negatives ("Don't use no double negatives").

But many other traditional grammatical rules are flouted daily and, in many instances, these violations result in livelier, clearer writing. (I just broke one. You should never start a sentence with a conjunction, and I don't think we— or the sentence in question—are any the worse for wear, are we?)

The Review and Polish step of my system proceeds from the assumption that the art has been achieved, to put it loftily. The Review and Polish step of this system proceeds from the assumption that the "art" has been created. Your message has been verbalized, and all that remains is to scrutinize, critique, repair, and polish your work.

You have done your research, compiled your notes, meticulously culled through vast quantities of ideas, questions, facts, images, random thoughts, and anything else you came across when researching your subject. You have written your table of contents, and from that outline, you have completed your book, article, speech, or term paper. You are fairly confident that what you have written achieves your goal: to tell your readers or listeners what you want them to know about the subject you have written about. You have built your house, you have painted or sided it, hell, you have even furnished it and gotten cable (and maybe DSL service) wired into every room.

Now is the time, however, when you must find the window that doesn't open all the way, the door that doesn't close right, the electrical outlet that doesn't work, the pipe that leaks, the carpet that's buckled in a certain spot, the step that creaks, the toilet that runs after you flush it, the burner on the stove that doesn't heat up, the cabinet drawer that sticks, the faucet that drips, the...well, I think you get the point.

It cannot be overemphasized how important it is to step back for a time before you review and polish your work. A change occurs in your writer's mind that allows you to see your writing through a different set of eyes. What was once brilliantly composed may perhaps seem clumsy and in need of tweaking. We tend to become immune to certain problems with our work while we're writing it. However reading your copy while writing it is a different process than reading your copy to make sure it's perfect. Let us assume you have given your work a little time to breathe before diving back into it.

Before you edit anything, you should print out a copy of the manuscript, if at all possible. For a lengthy book that you have written in its entirety on a computer, this may be unrealistic. However, for an article, speech, or paper, a hard copy is a good way to get an overall sense of the piece as it will read in printed form. Working on a computer screen can be somewhat numbing, with text-wrapping and the computer's seemingly endless lines of text. However, when you hold 10 or 20 pages of copy in your hand to read and edit, the piece comes to life and the necessary revisions become more apparent. I know a great many writers who have had this experience and have ended up making major changes in their work after seeing it printed out.

Whether or not you revise a printout or a file on your hard drive, one of the quickest and easiest ways to identify clumsy construction and bad flow is to read your work aloud, preferably in private. Right now *you* want to be the only one who hears your work; you are now in evaluation mode, and another person's opinion may muddy your judgment (*especially* if the listener is a loved one who thinks every word you write is gold by default).

So what should you listen for as you read aloud? And what should you be on the lookout for as you read silently?

Problems

These problems can include...

- **Sentences that don't seem to make sense.** When you wrote them they sounded great. Now they're convoluted and confusing. Fix them. Either rewrite them completely, or break the component parts into two or more sentences.

- **Adjectives and/or adverbs** that do not seem to be the right word for the intent of the qualification. Do not use "thrilling" if you mean "exhilarating." Do not use "honestly" when you mean "forthright." And on and on....

- **Split infinitives** (putting an adverb between "to" and the infinitive it governs). Sometimes it is extremely tempting to leave an infinitive split, simply because it ends up reading more naturally when you do. It's a judgment call, but be judicious in your use of split infinitives.

    As an exercise, which of the following sentences sounds more natural?

    We will show you how to carefully structure your work.

    or

    We will show you how to structure carefully your work.

    The second example is technically correct, but the first is more pleasing to the ear. Personally, I would have no problem splitting the construction "to" and "structure" with the adverb "carefully" to achieve the results of such a clearly understood sentence.

- **Redundancies.** Redundancies occur when you repeat something that you just said; that is, when you say the same thing more than once; or when you are carelessly repetitive and express an idea more than one time in the same paragraph or even (heaven forbid) in the same sentence. Redundancy should be avoided.

- **Cliches.** The bottom line is that cliches are old hat and you should avoid them like the plague and like there's no tomorrow. If you do, your writing will read like the cat's pajamas and your readers won't blow hot and cold when they eyeball your stuff. Paying attention to things like avoiding cliches could make you go from rags to riches because your readers will think you see eye to eye with them.

It's easy to be a Monday-morning quarterback when it comes to things like cliches, because it never rains but it pours when you let the cat out of the bag and use even one cliche. Cliches are a sticky wicket for editors, though, and you can argue for leaving them in until the cows come home, but I'll bet you dollars to doughnuts, you'll lose that battle and go down in flames. Then you'll have to batten down the hatches, eat humble pie, seize the bull by the horns, buckle down, and go back to the drawing board.

Even if it sets your teeth on edge, you'll have to go back to square one, start from scratch, not split hairs, snap to it, and see how the land lies until you see the light at the end of the tunnel and your writing is spic and span (even though rewriting your words was like rubbing salt in a wound). After all, you'll have the last laugh if your piece scores big time. Then your critics will be laughing out of the other side of their mouths! You'll be the big cheese then, even though you originally had a bee in your bonnet over the changes you had to make, some of which cut to the quick.

But you're no babe in the woods and every cloud has a silver lining, so bite your tongue, get off your high horse, let sleeping dogs lie, and get your act together. When all is said and done, you'll be happy as a clam and you'll sleep like a log.

- **Misspelled words.** Do *not* depend on your word processing program's spell-checker to check your text for spelling errors. As you'll see, the following poem makes this point quite effectively. (Thanks to my agent and writer extraordinaire, John White, for passing this along).

I have a spelling checker;
It came with my PC.
It plainly marks four my review
Mistakes I cannot sea.

I strike a key and type a word
And weight four it two say
Weather eye am wrong oar write.
It shows me strait a weigh.

As soon as a mist ache is maid
It nose bee fore two long
And eye can put the error rite.
Its rarely ever wrong.

I've run this poem threw it,
I'm sure yore pleased two no.
It's letter-perfect in its weigh—
My checker tolled me sew.

So bare with me, I due the best eye can.

- **Excessively long paragraphs.** Short, punchy paragraphs are easier to read, flow better, and are more visually appealing. Break up huge paragraphs into several smaller paragraphs (when feasible, of course) and your piece will immediately be livelier and more accessible.

- **Passive voice.** This is a tough problem to both identify and correct because many times there is a tendency to use the passive voice in both speaking and writing. Passive voice diminishes the power of nouns, however, and is far less direct. For instance, here are some examples of sentences written in both passive and active voice:

Passive	**Active**
The cars were covered with snow.	Snow covered the cars.
The reason she quit her job was because she didn't like her boss.	She quit her job because she did not like her boss.
The clock was struck.	The clock struck.

Sometimes, passive voice is appropriate. Which of the following two sentences are clearer?

Government officials released the incriminating documents yesterday.

or

The incriminating documents were released yesterday.

The second sentence is cleaner. Telling the reader that "government officials" released the documents is unnecessary and wordy. Watch for passive voice, but always make the final decision whether or not to rewrite based on clarity and directness of expression.

•••

This is not the forum for a comprehensive discussion of the essentials of grammar—there are countless books and Web sites that serve that purpose. In Appendix C on page 222, I suggest several valuable reference books that can assist you in identifying and correcting grammatical errors.

What I would like you to keep in mind for this step of the system is that, by the time you have reached this step, your work is essentially over. This step asks you to polish, not rebuild, your piece. So, try to defer to your original vision of the piece and consider your original words the stuff of merit and beauty.

Those words are not sacrosanct, of course. If you need to change something, by all means do so. But this is not the time to do a complete rewrite of your piece. If you have followed my system, then you have become an instant expert on the subject and, because your piece was constructed in phases, the final result should be very close to what you originally set out to do.

Unfortunately, there are exceptions to this rule: You may decide your book or article or speech or paper is so tragically flawed that it is irreparable. You reread and reread your copy, and decide you unequivocally hate what you have written. You will have to decide if you are going to scrap what you have done and start over, or reject your instinct that the piece is not fixable and fix it anyway.

If it comes to this, it will be your call…and I sincerely hope it never comes to that. The only thing I can suggest—if you decide that your worst fear has manifested itself and your piece is awful—is to start over. However, use the same Six Step System over again. You obviously did something wrong the first time around, so retrace your steps and do it right the second time. One way or another, you will get it done. (You will have to, after all.) Or you will give up. That is your decision and your choice. But allow me to make one last suggestion before I wrap this up: Do not give up.

To conclude, reflect on this piece of advice from the Hoosier writer and humorist Kin Hubbard:

There is no failure except in no longer trying. There is no defeat except from within, no really insurmountable barrier save our own inherent weakness of purpose.

Now go write your masterpiece.

section II

The Projects

chapter

The Projects:
An Introduction

 Nothing is a waste of time if you use the experience wisely.

—Rodin

Y ou are not going to be interested in how to give a speech if you want to write a book or a magazine article. And if you have a due date for a term paper, you probably don't care about much besides getting the paper done (especially if a significant portion of your grade depends on your paper).

But I suggest that you read this section in its entirety. You can go right to the chapter concerning your specific project now, but when it's convenient, read the other three chapters as well.

As I discuss each of these four very important, and very different creative writing forms—book, article, speech, and term paper—I will touch on factors relevant to all forms of writing, and provide a plethora of interesting and enlightening examples of techniques that can be applied universally to the creative act, regardless of what you are actually writing.

chapter 13

Lincoln Logs

> ❝ *You can write about anything, and if you write well enough, even the reader with no intrinsic interest in the subject will become involved.* ❞
>
> —**Tracy Kidder**

*T*here's an old adage that there is no better way of teaching than by example and so, in this book, I will walk you through the process of writing four works: a book, a speech, a magazine article, and a term paper.

I won't actually write the pieces, mind you, but I will show you how to assemble your research materials, how to selectively zero in on the information you will need to do the actual writing, how to put together your outline, and how to revise, edit, and rewrite so the piece is the best it can be.

There is another old adage that the three most written about subjects in the English language are the Civil War, Christ, and the Titanic. However, I would add one more subject to that short list: Abraham Lincoln. A recent search of Barnes & Noble's Web site (*bn.com*) came up with 342 titles related to Lincoln. That did not include the out-of-print stuff, much of which is still available through used book dealers. That also does not include the e-texts available on the Internet on sites such as Project

Guttenberg (*www.promo.net/pg*) which, last time I checked, had two public domain, full-blown biographies of Old Abe free for the asking.

So with this plethora of titles about Lincoln already out there, what are *we* going to write about in our fictitious, hypothetical masterpieces?

Why, Abraham Lincoln, of course.

We will look specifically at an aspect of Lincoln's life that often gets overlooked in the avalanche of words

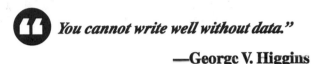 *You cannot write well without data."*

—George V. Higgins

written about the Civil War, the Emancipation Proclamation, the Gettysburg Address, slavery, his assassination, and his writings. We are going to focus on his children.

You will do the research and become an instant expert on Lincoln's children and you will evaluate how our 16th president should be graded as a parent.

Your vehicles for telling this tale will be the following four projects:

- Your **book** will be called *Robert, Willie, Eddie, & Tad: The Sons of Abraham Lincoln.*
- Your **magazine article** will be titled **"In His Own Right: Robert Todd Lincoln."**
- Your **speech** will be called **"Father Abe: Parenting Tips of Abraham Lincoln."**
- Your **term paper** will bear the title **"Robert Todd Lincoln: The Price of Having a Famous Father."**

The clock is ticking, deadlines are breathing down your neck...empires and careers hinge on your efforts, so it's Miller time!

Well, not really.

But I am not kidding about the pressing nature of deadlines, be they publisher deadlines, magazine lead-times, end of semester requirements, or the relentless stampede of days on the calendar as your speech date approaches.

The next chapter spells all this out in detail. Take a breath...and then let us proceed.

Tick Tock, Tick Tock...

> **Writer's block is a luxury most people with deadlines don't have.**
>
> —**Diane Ackerman**

kay, Mr. (or Mrs. or Ms.) Phelps. Pay attention. (The above line is my attempt to be clever by inserting an obscure *Mission: Impossible* reference into this chapter. But in my defense, there is a lesson here: If your reader does not get the reference, then your writing will be perceived as confusing. So be sure your witticisms are universal enough to be immediately recognized by the majority of your readers.)

These four projects and the process of writing each of them are very specific. If you are assigned the task of writing any one of these three "art forms" (and yes, writing is art) you may be tempted to jump to that section right away and ignore the rest of the book. Let me advise you to read *everything*. There is a great deal of important information and advice in the other sections of the book. It will be to your benefit if you read the speech section, even if you only have to write a term paper. Reading the term paper section could be a great help in writing a book...even if it has been 20 years since you have sat in a college classroom. I wouldn't want you

98

to overlook a valuable tip simply because you thought that a particular project did not apply to you. So, here is your situation:

The book

You, the writer, have a book contract with Spignesi Books of Scranton to write a book titled *Robert, Eddie, Willie, and Tad: The*

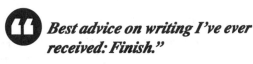

Best advice on writing I've ever received: Finish."

—Peter Mayle

Sons of Abraham Lincoln. You negotiate a $20,000 advance, half of which you will receive on signing the contract, and the remaining half on acceptance of the book. You have one year to research the data, write the book, and turn it in. You have agreed to write a book of between 150,000 and 200,000 words and to provide approximately 15 relevant photos (for which all rights, fees, and clearances are your responsibility). You must turn in two hard copies of the manuscript, plus a 3.5" floppy disk of the complete manuscript in either Mac or PC format.

The magazine article

You, the writer, have a contract with *Passion for the Past* magazine to write an article for their November issue called "In His Own Right: Robert Todd Lincoln." The article is to be 3,500 words (no more than 4,000) and your fee is $1,500: $500 on signing the agreement and the balance on acceptance. You have an August 1 deadline (approximately three months from when you sign the contract) to turn in the article. At least three photos of Robert Todd Lincoln at varying stages in his life must be turned in with the article (with all rights and clearances acquired).

The speech

You, the speaker, have agreed to deliver a speech of approximately 20 minutes in length called "Father Abe: Parenting Tips of Abraham Lincoln" at a seminar on parenting co-sponsored by the local Hospital of

St. Fabiola and Holden Caulfield University. Approximately 300 people will attend and you will be the fourth speaker on an agenda of eight. No visual material is required but there will be audiovisual equipment (a slide projector) at the auditorium if you choose to bring along slides to visually augment your talk. A 10-minute question-and-answer session will follow your speech for a total of 30 minutes on stage. There will be print media journalists present and the talks will be videotaped for archiving in the university library. You will not receive a fee for your presentation but lunch will be served and you will be allowed to hand out promotional materials (brochures, fliers, bibliographies, and so forth) if you have such items available for something you would like to promote.

The term paper

You, the student, are a political science major at Holden Caulfield University, and as part of your junior year American History course you must write a 10-page, 2,500- to 3,000-word term paper on some aspect of the American presidency. You have received instructor approval for a paper called **"Robert Todd Lincoln: The Price of Having a Presidential Father."** The paper must be in proper term paper form, complete with endnotes and a bibliography. The paper is due two weeks before your final exam, and after receiving approval for your topic a week after classes start, you have the majority of the 13 week semester to write your paper (approximately 10 weeks). Your paper is worth one quarter of your grade. The course's weekly quizzes, final, and your personal class participation (as evaluated by the instructor) comprise the other three quarters of your grade.

•••

When money, grades, reputation, and your impact on other people's schedules depend on whether or not you finish your writing, there is a shift in the way you need to think. Suddenly, there is pressure where before there was none.

It's not just a passion…it's a job.

I know people who work full time and write "on the side." Don't get me wrong: Many (if not most) of these scribes have a fully realized vision of the project they are working on—be it a screenplay, a book of advice, a novel, a collector's guide, or a biography. These writers have a passion for their subject and they *commit* to the project and give their all to doing the job right.

> *It's a job. It's not a hobby. You don't write the way you build a model airplane. You have to sit down and work, to schedule your time and to stick with it....If you're going to make writing succeed you have to approach it as a job."*
>
> **—Rosellen Brown**

But next month's mortgage payment probably does not depend on whether or not they fin-

> *Regarding writing:*
> *Find another profession to be young in."*
>
> **—Joe Queenan**

ish the book. A magazine editor probably won't be calling them every day asking when he or she can expect the final sections of an article. A convention won't be angry and disappointed if the part-time writer does not show up to present a speech on breast feeding. Nor will these writers fail an important, college-level course if they leave their work uncompleted. These writers can work on their projects in their spare time, at their leisure.

Invariably, the result of this limitless freedom is a more relaxed approach to the work, coupled with a willingness to drop the project for a vacation, a family function, or even for some overtime at work. (Or to watch *There's Something About Mary* on cable again.)

If you are one of those people, you will still find the approach to research delineated in this book useful. However, the core concepts that are the underpinning of this system— efficiency, timeliness, and meeting a deadline—are probably moot for your purposes. The techniques will still work, but you will probably find the repeated references to efficient use of your time and the omnipresent sense of urgency irrelevant.

For those of you who *do* have to meet deadlines, I hope you will find the tactics discussed in this book helpful. Like I said, time is a-pressin', so enough jibber-jabbering. And how do we begin? At the beginning.

chapter

Press Start

> **The difference between the right word and the almost right word is the difference between lightning and the lightning bug.**
>
> —**Mark Twain**

o, now that you know what is required of you, where do you begin? Even though it may end up changed, I always like to start with a title. (You might say it's my entitlement to do so.)

A *working title* (which may very well end up being your final title) gives you a handle, a focus, and a jumping-off point.

A working title eliminates the vague sense of "well, it's about..." and forces the researcher/writer to evaluate every piece of information he or she acquires from the perspective of, and within the context of, the title.

For example, if you are confused about your direction, you can ask yourself, "Does what I found further the premise of the piece? Or is it useless filler that was a waste of my valuable time?"

For instance, if, during your Lincoln research, you come across an accounting of the existing copies of the Gettysburg Address, but you happen to be the writer crafting the "Father Abe: Parenting..." speech, there is probably no way you're going to make much use of that information.

Although you could work an anecdote about the surviving documents into your introductory remarks and then try to tie it into the premise of the speech.

This example does not mean that there is no value in a wide range of reading when you're reviewing different texts and documents—it just means that you should not spend hours tracking down information that might ultimately result in an infinitesimally small contribution to your final work.

As discussed earlier, we have already determined—and equally importantly, titled —what we will be writing. (Turn to page 97 to review the titles of the projects.) All of these titles instantly convey a sense of the piece and will direct you towards the material you will need to write the four pieces.

Once you have decided on a working title, you can take the first steps on your research expedition. Your research will involve using the Internet, public and university libraries, and bookstores.

Honest Abe's Family in 6 Steps

This chapter provides detailed, specific illustrations on how to apply the Six Step System, using the fictitious projects about Abraham Lincoln's family as our model. As part of the Six Step process, every writer needs to ask the seven questions and work with the information they provide.

Step 1: Immersion

Applying the Immersion step of my system to a historical figure as monumental as Abraham Lincoln would seem to be an impossible task at first glance. Lincoln is one of the most studied and written about presidents in American history. To immerse yourself in Lincolnania could easily prove self-defeating as the books, articles, print-outs, videos, and other articles pile up. After a period of seeking out and compiling these materials, the writer will more than likely come to the realization that there is no way to use all of this stuff!

So what to do?

Improvise. And you can do that by applying what I call "selective immersion" to the process.

Firstly, you will need to get a sense of the Lincoln landscape. This preliminary step involves determining what books are available and which ones are most important; what is the range of available articles, academic journal essays, and materials from Web sites; and what Lincoln documentaries are readily accessible for rental.

After all that is accomplished, the selective elimination process can begin. Hopefully, your final list of items will be the most important...and the most useful. An obscure volume about Lincoln's political campaigns or a photo book of Civil War images may be interesting, but probably won't be much use to you. Be merciless in your selections. Remember, you have a finite amount of time and you should not use time you have scheduled for writing for the research process.

So cut, cut, cut your master list of source materials, always keeping your topic in mind and always staying focused on your goals for your work.

The 7 Questions

Who?

The answers to the question of "who?" for our Lincoln projects are Abraham Lincoln, his wife, Mary Todd Lincoln, and his four sons, Willie, Eddie, Tad, and Robert. As we do our research, we will find other characters in the pageant of the Lincolns' lives who played a role or are important in some other way, but you would begin with researching the principal players of your drama.

What?

In the case of Lincoln's sons, we are writing about a great many more things than just their name, rank, and serial number. We are researching and writing about:

- Abraham and Mary Lincoln as parents.
- The price a child pays for being the son of someone famous.
- What a family goes through when a young child dies.
- How children react to the murder of their father.
- What a son goes through having to testify against his mother and ultimately agreeing to have her committed.
- The significance and influence of Abraham Lincoln as a leader, a president, a parent, and a man.

In the story of Lincoln's sons, you have a rich subtext of powerful and emotional subjects, as well as a panoply of gripping stories set against the background of the period before the Civil War.

When

While doing the basic research for our "Lincoln's sons" pieces, we would learn that Mary and Abraham Lincoln's first son Robert was born on August 1, 1843. Their fourth and final son, Tad, was born on April 4, 1853—a span of only 10 years. From their birthdates alone, we can immediately identify the time period of our story as the mid-19th century.

For this aspect of our research, let's start with a stroll through *The People's Chronology* by James Trager. This exhaustive reference (a must for any writer's library—see the list of recommended references in Appendix C for more suggestions) lists dozens of global historical events in thirty categories, ranging from political events and exploration through theater, marine resources, and religion (and everything in between), in a very easy to use timeline format.

Looking at Robert Todd Lincoln's birth year of 1843, we would immediately discover that Boston schoolteacher Dorothea Dix revealed publicly for the first time the inhumane treatment of mental patients in Massachusetts state institutions. When we consider that more than 30 years later, the Lincoln son born in 1843 would help to have his mother declared insane and institutionalized, the value and gravity of this fact becomes obvious.

Where?

For our hypothetical Lincoln projects, we will need to learn about Springfield, Ill., Washington, D.C., as well as many towns that were ravaged by the Civil War.

Utilizing the Immersion approach to research, I would want to know about daily life in these places. Where did the residents buy their food? What were the outhouses like? What was the weather like? What happened when it rained? Did the streets become quagmires of mud? How did people get around town? Did they ride horses? Did they walk? Did every household have a coach or a buggy? What did residents do with their trash? Were people's clothes always dirty?

The answers to these questions will provide us with colorful details that will add life, vigor, and atmosphere to our writing. Again, specificity is key. Tell your readers how the wooden door of the privy closed—was it a hook and eye? A sliding bolt? A swinging board and a stop?

Why?

For our Lincoln projects, we can ask our "why?" question as an attempt to answer several key questions.

- Why did Eddie Lincoln die so young?
- Why did Robert Lincoln testify against his mother at her sanity trial?
- Why did Abraham Lincoln often leave his family for months at a time to work in Washington?
- Why did the Lincolns allow their sons to run roughshod over them, seemingly completely undisciplined?
- Why was Robert's body left unburied in a cemetery vault for two years?

How?

The goal of asking "how?" in your Lincoln research is to better understand relevant events, people's actions, and ancillary historical proceedings.

For instance, consider asking why Robert Lincoln agreed to have his mother committed naturally leads to the question of how he came to the decision to testify against her and how the courts ruled against her.

By answering this query, you will inevitably come upon remarks from Robert Lincoln and his mother, court findings, newspaper articles and editorials, and more, all related to the subject at hand. This serves to help your reader acquire a fuller, more complete understanding of your topic.

Weird?

For example, take our "Lincoln's sons" projects. In addition to reading the biographies and perusing the Web sites and digging through references for the facts you'll need to write your piece, we should also track down some magazines and newspapers (often available on the Internet) from the period in which Lincoln and his boys were alive and read some of the classified ads and editorials from these publications. These "of the moment" curios can often illuminate what it was like during a time and then, hopefully, your writer's mind will digest this information and use it for anecdotal color or to add authoritative insight to your work.

In the case of our study of Lincoln's sons, what unusual information will we uncover in our research? (I peeked ahead.)

How about the fact that the corpse of Robert Todd Lincoln, Lincoln's eldest son, remained in a receiving vault at Dellwood Cemetery in Hildene, Vermont, for two years following his death, and that when he was finally interred, Robert was buried in Arlington National Cemetery instead of in the Lincoln family tomb at Springfield, Illinois. As Ruth Randall wrote in her biography, *Lincoln's Sons,* "One does not know the why of this...or whose decision it was."

This is weird information, and we can definitely use it.

Step 2: Notes

Look at the following list of notes. For the four projects we are working on, my initial list of notes topics would look like this. Note that each of these bulleted points is a relevant area of information that needs to be explored:

- birth info of each boy (date, time, place, etc.)
- health of sons at birth
- what was childbirth like in the mid-1800s? sidebar?
- find Lincoln quotes about his sons—go through bios and books of collected writings
- look for anything that can be reprinted in its entirety?
- check Mary Todd bios for her quotes about sons
- Robert's accomplishments—important businessman—Pullman Company
- military careers of Eddie and Robert? (Only?)
- Tad the youngest - hellion?
- photos
- Mary Todd Lincoln's insanity trial
- trial transcripts?
- original newspaper accounts of trial?
- *New York Times* articles about Robert? (does *Times* index go back that far?)
- interviews with Robert
- letters from sons (public domain by now?)
- where did family live during the boys' childhood?
- photos of homes
- Lincoln's grandchildren
- family tree?
- bios of Lincoln's daughters-in-law
- suggested reading
- Web sites list
- Lincoln organizations
- find local Lincoln experts to interview—Yale?
- birth certificates
- school records
- find as many quotes by sons (*confirmed* quotes) as possible

Taking notes is admittedly a tedious process. It takes a great deal of work to research the information listed, yet it is also one of the most fascinating parts of the job of writing a book, article, speech, or paper. You will learn a great deal during this phase, not only about your subject, but also about how you interpret the topic and what you ultimately want to say about it.

At the conclusion of the note-taking process, you will have the heart of your piece. You then can step back and review the material and think through the different aspects of the subject.

Step 3: Review and Think

For our Lincoln projects, I would apply the same criteria in order to make critical decisions about including or rejecting items. Eventually, I would refine the list down to a workable list of topics. All of these topics would then need to be further explored and written about. This hand-picked list of topic points is, in essence, your working table of contents.

Step 4: Table of Contents

What would a table of contents for *Robert, Eddie, Willie, and Tad: The Sons of Abraham Lincoln* look like? What would be included? How long would it/should it be?

For a biography such as this, there are some choices to be made. If the book will be in chronological order, should it begin with the marriage of Mary Todd and Abraham Lincoln, continuing through the births of all four sons, and concluding with the death of their last son? Or should we use a thematic structure for the book?

This incident-driven treatment would require chapters, in no particular chronological order, about each son and his character and doings. It would also include chapters on the Civil War, Lincoln's presidency, Mary Todd and her eventual mental collapse, and so on. All of the chapters' themes would have been decided upon based on your research and your individual ideas about the material you uncovered. For a book structured in this manner, an appendix consisting of a detailed timeline is often useful to anchor the events recounted in the book in the minds of your readers and add historical accuracy to the book. These decisions are yours to make.

If I were writing this book, I would probably choose to do it in chronological order. I have always liked the tidy structure of a narrative that begins in a certain year and ends in a certain year.

However, this is *my* interpretation of how to write this story and it would be up to you to decide what the structure of your own book should be. This is why the working table of contents is such an important step in the process of writing a book (or any of the other projects we have been discussing).

Again, with a working table of contents, you can move things around, delete and add things, change the title of sections, and see the entire book at a glance. This is always extremely helpful and leads quite nicely into the next step of the writing process: the Chapter-by-Chapter phase of the six step system.

In fact, once you have the table of contents as close to complete as it can be, you can then even figure out how long each chapter must be.

After becoming an expert on the lives of Lincoln's sons, and carefully thinking through the layout of the book, let's assume that you have determined that you need 18 chapters to recount the life stories of Abe's boys. After completing the working table of contents, you also know the working titles of each chapter as well. Now let's add an introduction, a bibliography, an afterword, and an index to those 18 chapters. Also, let's say you have your sights set on a final total of 175,000 words for the book which is a compromise between the low end of the contract word requirement (150,000 words) and the high end (200,000 words).

Therefore, you know that you will have 163,000 words in which to write your 18 chapters (an average of 9,000 words per chapter). I use the word *average* intentionally. Undoubtedly, there will be chapters that you will be able to write adequately with half that number of words. There will be chapters that require twice those words to do the material justice.

This scheduling process can be applied to the other projects we have discussed—an article, speech, and term paper—but because a book requires the largest amount of work and takes the most time to write, mapping out your time for the project is somewhat more important than it is for less demanding, short-term projects.

You can determine what is important for the purposes of your work, only by compiling and reviewing a staggering amount of information about a subject. Then, you can decide on what you want to write about.

When you create your table of contents, you don't need to worry about finalizing the precise title of each chapter. There will always be time for revising and refining. In the initial stages of the contents phase, simply write down a chapter title that describes the chapter's focus.

For instance, for our Lincoln's sons book, I would probably start with Abraham and Mary Todd Lincoln's marriage. Because the book is concentrating on the sons, it would seem out of place to include a great deal of biographical material on Lincoln or his wife. That's fodder for another book.

So, let's title Chapter 1 "The Marriage of Abraham and Mary." Chapter 2 could be "The Happy Couple's Early Years." Chapter 3 could be "A Baby in the House." Chapter 4 could be "Robert Gets a Brother." Continue working your way through a chronological look at the Lincolns and their sons, until you have completed the working table of contents.

As you will recall, we are using a book called *Lincoln's Sons*, by Ruth Painter Randall, as a source. This book is now out-of-print, but still available. Ms. Randall chose to write her book with a thematic structure. The titles of the first six chapters of Randall's book are:

- A Family on Eighth Street.
- The First Two "Dear Codgers."
- Two More "Blessed Fellows."
- Growing Up in Springfield.
- "Me and Father."
- "Our Eldest Boy, Bob...Promises Very Well."

One can easily see how the author constructed her book using incidents from the lives of the Lincolns and their sons, instead of beginning with their marriage and moving chronologically through the births of the sons along with subsequent events.

Both approaches are valid and it is the author's determination as to which to use. This important decision will reflect his or her ultimate vision of the work.

Step 5: Chapter by Chapter

Sometimes that point is multifaceted. As in the case of our hypothetical book about Lincoln's sons, we will present a great deal of information about the lives of Abe's four boys. We will make individual points about each son and their life based on our research and our interpretation of the facts.

For the magazine article about Robert Todd Lincoln, our thesis might be that Robert Lincoln was his own man and lived a rich and rewarding life, accomplishing a great many things that had nothing to do with the fact that his father was Abraham Lincoln.

For the speech, our point might be that sometimes Abraham Lincoln was unable to be a participatory father in his children's lives because of the demands of his career. This allowed the bulk of the job of raising his sons to fall on his wife…with the subsequent consequences spelled out later.

For the term paper, our thesis might be that having a presidential father does not always translate into the reaping of benefits throughout life, and that, in many cases, it can be a detriment to living a fulfilling life because in the eyes of society, the family, and the country, the child is always in the shadow of his father, the president.

Step 6: Review and Polish

This step is very straightforward: Read through your draft work, review for style, content, form, tone, etc., and edit as needed. And once this is done, polish your work with a soft touch, tightening, cleaning up awkward constructions, breaking wordy sentences into two or more sentences, and so forth. At this point, you want to make your work as pleasurable to read as possible.

The Book

A book is the only place in which you can examine a fragile thought without breaking it, or explore an explosive idea without fear it will go off in your face...It is one of the few havens remaining where a man's mind can get both provocation and privacy.

—**Edward P. Morgan**

Provocation and privacy." I like that. Is there a better shorthand description of what a book provides? There is no other artistic creation wrought by the hand and mind of man that compares with the book. I still remember the day of my first book sale, a day that is one of the most memorable in a writer's life.

The excitement and explosive glee is overwhelming and the first thing you want to do is tell someone. And I did. I called my cousin Dan, who is also a close friend, and told him that I had sold my first book. Fifteen years and 20 books later, I dedicated my *Beatles Book of Lists* to him:

> *From me to...My cousin Dan Fasano, a totally devoted Beatlefan who completely understands why Paul's bass line in "Dear Prudence" is a subject worthy of at least a half hour's discussion— even if the phone's ringing, the kids are screaming, and it's starting to rain with all the windows open.*

I sold *Mayberry, My Home Town* in 1984; it was published three years later in 1987. As I have said previously, that book leaped into my mind in a heartbeat. The three years between signing the contract and the finished product simply involved putting the words (the *right* words, of course) on paper.

This is not always the case. This kind of Zen-like visualization/realization of a book before it exists is not always how books come into being: In fact, I am sorry to say, these moments of clarity are the exception, not the rule.

And this brings us to a discussion of a key question: What is a book? Here's a definition I use and that I have found useful: "A book is a collection of ideas and information put forth in a context which proceeds from the author's unique point of view on the subject." The key words in this definition are "collection," "ideas and information," and "author's unique point of view."

A book is unlike a magazine article, which explores one facet of a subject; a speech, which is even more narrow; or a term paper, which is meant to prove to an instructor that you have learned something, and that you have an opinion about a certain aspect of the material covered that semester.

> **When you sell a man a book you don't sell him just 12 ounces of paper and ink and glue—you sell him a whole new life."**
>
> **—Christopher Morley**

From the early days of hand-inked illuminated manuscripts to today's digital e-books, books have been a special—perhaps even hallowed—form of self-expression. And as long as humankind continues to exist and continues to form opinions, books will continue to be the single most important forum for the concise, portable, and lasting expression of ideas.

So what is a book?

So what, then, is the essence of a book? What do you need to know before you tackle the writing of a nonfiction book —aside from mountains of info about your subject, of course?

First, here are some parameters. A nonfiction book can range from less than 40,000 words up to a million words or more. The Bible is in the range of a million words, depending on the translation. The complete works of William Shakespeare (which are often collected in a single volume) comprise about 1.5 million words. My biggest book, *The Complete Stephen King Encyclopedia*, is 750,000 words, (My shortest book, *Gems, Jewels, and Treasures*, is approximately 25,000 words.

Here are some examples from the past few years of a range of non-fiction books (including some of mine) and their approximate lengths (in descending order):

- *The Oxford Companion to American Military History* edited by John Whiteclay Chambers II (Oxford University Press): **1,100,000 words.**
- *The Complete Book of U. S. Presidents* by William A. DeGregorio (Barricade Books): **365,000 words.**
- *Lincoln* by David Herbert Donald (Simon & Schuster): **315,000 words.**
- *Italian Neighbors, or A Lapsed Anglo-Saxon in Verona* by Tim Parks (Grove Weidenfeld): **115,000 words.**
- *The Italian 100: A Ranking of the Most Influential, Cultural, Scientific, and Political Figures, Past and Present* by Stephen J. Spignesi (Citadel Press): **110,000 words.**
- *Big Secrets: The Uncensored Truth About All Sorts of Stuff You Are Never Supposed to Know* by William Poundstone (Quill): **90,000 words.**
- *Lavender Lists: New Lists About Lesbian and Gay Culture, History, and Personalities* by Lynne Yamaguchi Fletcher and Adrien Saks (Alyson Publications): **65,000 words.**
- *JFK Jr.* by Stephen J. Spignesi (Citadel Press): **50,000 words.**
- *The Garfield Book of Cat Names* by Jim Davis (Ballantine Books): **15,000 words.**

As this list illustrates, books are a wonderfully adaptable and extremely flexible art form. Books can be as long or as short as you want (within reason, of course). The format of the book is as consistently indulgent and accommodating as its creator is.

But this is not always a good thing. There is a huge difference between the open-ended format of a book indulging the artistic needs of the author. Note that I said "needs," not "whims.") An author who is self-indulgent shows reckless disregard for the reader. This is why God created editors.

> *I want the reader to turn the page and keep on turning to the end. This is accomplished only when the narrative moves steadily ahead, not when it comes to a weary standstill, overloaded with every item uncovered in the research."*
>
> **—Barbara Tuchman**

Even though there will always be a "literary firewall" (or the critiquing editor) standing between a book with problems and its publication, it is the author's *job* to turn in the best manuscript possible. It should be a tome that epitomizes the book's raison d'etre. It should be a collection of pages that says precisely what the author wanted to say when he or she first came up with the idea for the book—and says it using the precise number of words necessary to do the job right.

You as your own marketing department

Years ago, I taught a seminar for writers on how to market their work. My system required researching publishers to find the ones that would be interested in a writer's particular project. I showed how to write and send out multiple query letters and then follow up with the right samples, outlines, and other materials to make the submission process as efficient as possible. Hopefully, this will improve the writer's chances as much as possible. (See Chapter 22 for more details on this system.)

But before a single query letter was mailed, the first thing I had my students do was identify their readers. Of course it's a given that different people read different books, but not all at once. Thus, when a person goes into a bookstore looking for a book on fly fishing or a dessert cookbook, he or she wants to find books about fly fishing in the sports department of the store, and the dessert cookbooks in the cookbook department.

As an exercise to determine this critical fact, I asked my students to tell me which department of the bookstore their book would be shelved in. This was often a revelatory experience for many beginning writers. For the first time, they were being forced to confront their book and *define it.*

Military histories (or books about fly fishing) are not going to be displayed with cookbooks, Books about UFOs are not going to be found in the bridal section. A literary critique of the work of Willa Cather is not going to be shelved with the business books.

One student described her book to me with this blurb: "It's about when I helped my sister through her abortion and how she went back to the Roman Catholic Church after it was all over." By asking her the following questions, I talked her through the process of placing her book in the appropriate department of a bookstore:

- Did it belong in the **psychology** department? (The emotional trauma of abortion.)

- Did it belong in the **religion** department? (The value of spirituality during a personal crisis.)

- Did it belong in the **women's issues** department? (The difficulty of finding an abortion provider in a conservative state.)

- Did it belong in the **medical** department? (The impact the abortion had on her sister's reproductive system.)

- Did it belong in the **humor** department? ("How my twisted sense of humor helped my sister through the most difficult time of her life.") Don't automatically dismiss this possibility as farfetched: *Saturday Night Live* comedienne Julia Sweeney wrote and starred in a hilarious one-woman show called *God Said Ha!*, which was about her brother's death from cancer…at a time when she was diagnosed with uterine cancer.

- Did it belong in the **personal memoirs/autobiography** department? ("This is the story of my family and especially my sister and what happened to her.")

Books are usually identified (and marketed) by categories, and defining your reader will usually assist you in fitting your book with a category. In my student's case, she said yes to every question, which led me (and her) to conclude that the book's focus was too diffuse and her thesis was too vague. Granted, the book may have touched on all the issues I described. Unfortunately, the book cannot be in every department of the bookstore. What the writer needed to do was re-evaluate her book and determine which of them was the strongest. Then she needed to decide where the book belonged (and punch up/revise/rewrite as needed to give the book a stronger focus).

In addition, the publisher's sales team will need a one-line description of your book in order to sell it to bookstore buyers. By defining your audience, you can often arrive at a shorthand description of the book that will help bring it to the attention of the perfect reader for your book.

The following list consists of some examples of how some fictitious books might be described at a sales conference, and in which department of a bookstore these books might eventually find a home.

You will notice that some books listed here have more than one bookstore department listed. These are the titles that would easily fit in more than one category, although it would be a judgment call on the part of the bookstore as to where to put the title in question.

There is invariably some overlap in bookstore categories. And, all our talk of pinpointing a book's category aside, sometimes a book will fit quite nicely in more than one category, and would probably do well in either.

For instance, a book about the Salem witch trials could be shelved in either the American history, law, or new age sections. In this case, the bookstore staff would probably decide based on which of these three departments got the most traffic in their store.

Also, it is not uncommon for similar subjects to be grouped under one umbrella category. For example, UFO books are often found in a general new age section when the store does not have an UFO section. The reality of all this is that sometimes, selling books is more an art than a science.

In the case of Internet bookstores, this kind of categorizing is not an issue, because computers allow a retailer to list a book in as many categories as desired, simply because sites such as Amazon.com do not deal with the books themselves in their e-tailing environment. However, bookstores do not have that luxury and, in any case, defining your book with as much specificity as possible can only help make it a better book anyway.

To give you an idea on how books are displayed here is a list of books from "Hypothetical Books, Inc." and where you might find them in a bookstore:

- A Barbie doll price guide **(collectibles).**
- A biography of Abraham Lincoln's four sons **(biography, American history).**
- A book about foot fetishism **(sexuality).**
- A book about how to prepare for the SAT or ACT **(study guides).**
- A book about Renaissance paintings **(art).**
- A book about the HBO series *The Sopranos* **(television).**
- A book compiling phone numbers, addresses, Web sites, e-mail addresses, and other contact info for every U.S. government agency **(reference).**
- A book of medical questions and answers **(medical)**.
- A book of positive, uplifting sayings and stories **(motivation/self-help)**.
- A catalog of weapons used by American armed forces during the Korean War **(military history).**
- A collection of interviews with basketball personalities **(sports, basketball).**
- A collection of Monica Lewinsky jokes **(humor, American history, contemporary issues, sexuality, media studies).**
- A collection of photographs of nudes by several acclaimed photographers **(photography).**
- A complete history of the Salem witch trials **(new age, American history, law).**
- A comprehensive history of the sinking of the Titanic, with period documents and photos **(nautical history, British history, transportation).**

- A detailed traveler's guide to the landmarks of Venice, Rome, Florence, and Naples **(travel).**
- A fun look at the films of Harrison Ford, with interviews and photos **(movies).**
- A handbook for first-time cat owners **(pets).**
- A history of UFO sightings in New England **(new age, occult, UFOs, regional).**
- A legal handbook for landlords **(law).**
- A pasta cookbook that does not have a single recipe that uses tomatoes **(cookbooks).**
- A "sex for seniors" handbook **(sexuality, senior citizens)**.
- A study of sunspots and their effect on telecommunications **(astronomy, science).**
- A study of the works of George Gershwin **(music).**
- An encyclopedia of mammals **(natural history, zoology, animals, reference).**
- An insightful discussion of the nature of creativity, written by a clinical psychologist who is also an acclaimed painter and sculptor **(psychology, art).**
- Great vegetables for apartment dwellers to grow **(gardening)**.
- Macintosh iBook tips and secrets **(computers).**
- Successful dotcom strategies for beginners **(business, computers).**
- The complete score of *Cats* **(music, Broadway).**

Ideally, you will have determined the category of your book during the research and writing process. (This should include a visit to a major bookstore.) When browsing the categories in the store, you should also look for books that are on the same subject as what you want to write about. Being aware of the competition is often an effective way to shape your own book into something that will compete effectively and not be rejected automatically "because so and so did a book like that six months ago."

As part of the process, you will, at some point, have decided on a title for the book and drafted a working outline, which will eventually be expanded and refined into the table of contents (even if the final book does not offer a table of contents).

A nonfiction book should not be formulaic. However, its format should follow a formula, or, better, have a structure that is part of the accepted format for books. The better organized your material, the more accessible your book will be to your reader. Lately, the publishing industry has been trying to push the envelope in the way books are designed and structured. Sometimes it seems as though publishers are trying to compete with television and the Internet and magazines by creating books that are visually "aggressive" and nontraditionally structured.

I saw one hardcover book recently that was line after line of text on different colored pages with no margins. Photos and graphics were embedded in the body of the text so haphazardly that you could not tell where a line of text jumped to on the page. I do not remember what the book was about because I got a headache by just flipping through it.

Regardless of a book's design, the ultimate essence of a book is words on paper. Anything that hinders the easy processing of the writer's words by the reader seems to me to be akin to offering someone a steak…and only a spoon with which to eat. It *can* be done, but it sure does make it more difficult to eat—and takes away a great deal of the enjoyment.

But the reason people love movies such as *The Godfather, Citizen Kane, Annie Hall*, or *Alien* is because they have a beginning, a middle, and an end. And that is what your book should have, be it fiction or nonfiction. Outline and structure your books in a linear, logical, coherent way and you will be assuring accessibility. Sometimes a disjointed structure can assist the flow of a story. Take *Pulp Fiction*, for example. Directory Quentin Tarantino bent the rules of plot structure and still guaranteed coherence. But sometimes, a disjointed structure is just *bad* structure.

For the purposes of our discussion, let us go back to working on our hypothetical book: *Robert, Eddie, Willie, and Tad: The Sons of Abraham Lincoln*. But first, let's identify the department of the bookstore where this book would find a home.

The first and most logical choice would be biography, if the bookstore has a biography department. Some stores put biographies of the people involved in a field in the department with which the person was most associated. For example, some stores would put a biography of Carl Sagan in the science department; a bio of Mother Teresa in religion, a bio of Sandra Bullock in film, a bio of Adolf Hitler in World War II or military history, and a bio of John Lennon in music. Therefore, the second category choice for our "Lincoln's Sons" book would be American history.

Now let's figure out how long our book will be. This one's easy, because our publisher has already decided the book should be between 150,000 and 200,000 words…and you signed a contract agreeing to this word count.

You now have your title, word count, the category the book belongs in, and, if you have diligently followed my Six Step System, you will have pages of research materials. These pages should include:

- **Primary sources**, documents from the period, including writings by Abraham and Mary Lincoln, newspaper articles, books from the period, among others.
- **Secondary sources** everything else written about the subject that you think might be relevant.
- **Reviews of books** written about the Lincolns.
- **Books and articles** on the Civil War, the time period of the Lincolns and their children, and other possibly useful materials.

There will be papers, articles, books, letters, speeches, and other texts in your research findings that will not serve to further your understanding of the lives and times of the sons of Abraham Lincoln. For example, a letter from Lincoln to Ulysses S. Grant would not seem to contain any useful information within this context. Yet, spot-reading or scanning such documents is a fine way of acquiring a sense of both the personalities involved as well as the tenor of the times. Do not dismiss a document simply because something about your topic does not leap off the page at you at first glance. Take a stroll through the piece…but do it quickly. You never know what you might find.

The particular Lincoln letter I referred to previously is dated July 13, 1863. It consists of Lincoln thanking Grant for "the almost inestimable service you have done the country." Lincoln goes on to admit that he thought that one of Grant's troop movement decisions concerning the taking of Port Gibson and vicinity had been a mistake. The president concludes his brief missive stating that, "I now wish to make the personal acknowledgment that you were right and I was wrong."

This has nothing to do with Lincoln's sons, but it has an enormous amount to do with Lincoln himself. We learn Abraham Lincoln was a man who was not afraid to admit that he made a mistake. This is especially revealing and we would keep this in mind as we studied Lincoln's sons and their relationship and interaction with their parents.

It is truly an honorable man who can admit when he is wrong and it would be interesting to your readers to find an incident in which Abraham Lincoln admitted a mistake to one of his sons—and then cite this letter to Grant as another example of the kind of character with which Lincoln tried to raise his boys.

After your careful review and study of your research materials, you will have made the rough Lincoln's sons notes list (a sample list of these kinds of notes and queries is in the section on notes), and after the Review and Think step, you will have drafted a working table of contents, even if, as we have discussed, the book (or other work) will not ultimately feature a table of contents.

The next step is the actual Chapter by Chapter writing of the book. As I discussed previously, you already know that your book will be 18 chapters long, and you also know approximately how long each chapter should be.

I have always found it extremely useful to keep a running total of the words written for each of my books as I write them. My way of doing this is to create a two-column table listing each chapter separately. (Even if you have not finalized the chapters' titles, you can still create a cell for each chapter, using "Chapter 1," "Chapter 2," and so on.) In the adjacent column to the chapter, I put the word count of that chapter, which I ascertain using Microsoft Word's word count feature every time I add material to the chapter. (All word processing software packages feature this function—use it.) On a regular basis, I total up the words in the word count column of my table and, voila!, I have a running total of the number of words of the manuscript I have written so far.

I also find it useful to take this a step further and create a formula at the bottom of the page detailing the number of words written calculated as a percentage of the total words required:

$$\frac{46{,}716 \text{ words written}}{175{,}000 \text{ words required}} = 26.69\% \text{ completed}$$

You will be astonished at how helpful you will find this simple procedure. At a glance, you will know precisely where you are in the book and how much you have to do to finish it on time.

By monitoring your progress and production and keeping an eye on the calendar, you can know on an ongoing basis if you are working too slowly. And, if so, you can then compensate accordingly.

Deadlines in contracts are no joke. In fact, one publisher I worked for codified the seriousness of the due date by inserting lines in the contract that stated that timely delivery of the manuscript was the most important condition of the deal.

So, take a cue from CNN and The Weather Channel and give yourself constant updates. This way you can always be sure you are meeting your goals...and ultimately meet your deadline.

Once you have completed the writing of your book, you need to reread it and revise it. But the following is critically important: Do not begin rereading and revising immediately upon finishing the writing of the manuscript.

Allow yourself at least one night's sleep (preferably more) between you and the revision. You need to change your thought processes from that of a writer to that of a reader/editor...and that transformation takes time. One writer I know will not begin the revision process for at least a week after he has finished the writing of a manuscript. If you are pressed for time and cannot afford a week, at least wait a day or two.

In an ineffable way, your perception of your work will change. You will become "someone else" as you read through what you've written, and you will find problems with much of what you originally thought was final. Be judicious with what you change, but do pay attention to your response to the work. What has happened is that you have metamorphosed from a *writer* to a *reader*, and you will respond to your work as though it has been written by someone else.

What you thought was warm and nostalgic when you wrote it will appear as trite and corny. What you thought was clever and ironic will read as arrogant and unnecessary. What you thought as insightful and well-written will come across as confusing and convoluted. But do not completely surrender to the inner voice that now despises what you at first though was terrific.

Take this example from TV and popular culture: Talk-show host Rosie O'Donnell's personality is brash, boisterous, funny, and unaffected when she hosts her own show. Rosie is loud and animated and her fans absolutely adore her for it.

In May 2000, Rosie, who admits that she never watches her own show (it's done live and she never reviews the tape after the show) appeared for three nights as a celebrity guest on the incredibly popular ABC game show *Who Wants To Be a Millionaire*? On the day after her appearance, O'Donnell co-hosted *Live with Regis and Kathie Lee* and told host Regis Philbin that she had watched her appearance on the *Millionaire* show and was appalled by her loud and obnoxious behavior on the show. She said that if she were a stranger, she might actually write a nasty letter blasting her for her boisterous and uncouth ways.

Here's the point of all this: Almost everyone who saw Rosie on *Millionaire* (including Regis himself, it seems) thought Rosie was funny, personable, and an asset to the show. The truth is that Rosie was too harsh on herself and overly critical of her perfectly fine performance.

When it comes to your book, you initially thought that what you were writing was worthy of committing to paper. Always keep that in mind when you make your decisions as to what to revise, rewrite, or throw out all together.

Regarding this editorial revision process, I am not speaking of spot-revisions that you make as you write. Many writers rearrange sentences and rewrite passages for clarity during the actual writing, thanks to word processing software that allows instantaneous editing. This is not the same as beginning at the beginning of a manuscript and rereading and revising for a second draft. These two acts are different and, although each writer varies his or her writing practices, try and get through the writing of the entire manuscript before going back to page one and, in a sense, starting over.

Once you are happy with the final version of your text, the last stages of completing a book are mainly procedural. These include:

- **Printing out the manuscript.** Be sure there is a header in the upper left hand corner of each page with the title of the book and your last name. Also be sure each page is consecutively numbered. The title page (which you do not put a number on) is page 1. The next page is page 2, etc. Every page gets numbered, including the dedication, bibliography, and about the author. Put the approximate total word count of the manuscript in the upper right hand corner of the manuscript's title page.

- **Preparing a disk copy of the manuscript.** Hard copy submissions are required, but a disk (or disks) containing your manuscript in a standard format *is* more important than the paper copy.

    If you have a magazine article or book contract, be sure to read it carefully for formatting restrictions and other pertinent information for electronic submission. Most publishers can read both IBM and Macintosh disks today, but they may want a manuscript in a specific format (such as Microsoft Word, Corel WordPerfect, rich text format, plain text, and so on). Abide by these restrictions. It will make your editor's job easier and it will speed up the publication process. And if you wish to make a chart, be sure not to overly format it—you'll be wasting your time…and your editor's time. Your editor will have to reformat it anyway…and will end up griping about it for hours. Do everyone a favor and send your stuff formatted the way your editor wants it…or (better yet) don't format it at all.

- **Shipping the manuscript.** Send it sturdily packaged and wrapped. If you use FedEx or UPS, send it next day or second day. If you send it through the U.S. Postal Service, send it certified, return receipt requested.

•••

And there is one more, final step to completing a book: Have your next one conceptualized and waiting in the wings to begin researching right away, although a short respite of R & R is allowed. But writers write. So take a breather and then get started all over again!

The publishing eRevolution

Before I end this chapter, I must discuss the digital revolution that is occurring in publishing today. I know that there are those who decry the increasing prevalence of e-books (that is, digital texts that are downloaded off the Internet and read on a computer or a hand-held device, or are printed out). These naysayers—which some computer enthusiasts have decreed to be digital age Luddites—feel that books need to be held in the hand, opened and closed, and carried around in order for them to *really* be considered books. I am a dissenter to that school of thought (although I have never, to the best of my recollection, called somebody a Luddite).

I have engaged in this argument over "form vs. function" for years. I know people who will not listen to an incredible song or some other piece of music if they cannot hear it in stereo. That to me is like refusing to partake of an incredibly delicious delicacy simply because you have to eat it off a paper plate.

I'll admit that "Hey Jude" sounds better when heard off a remastered CD on a superb stereo system, but let's not lose sight of the big picture. "Hey Jude" is such a transcendent piece of songwriting that its beauty can be appreciated on a tinny transistor radio. And let's face it: Mozart heard on the same plastic radio is still Mozart.

This is an ongoing topic of discussion in the field of books and literature, too, and no less a literary luminary than Stephen King himself has weighed in on this debate.

In the field of King collecting, there are those fans who will buy an expensive limited edition of one of King's books and never read it. In fact, some will go so far as to refuse to remove the shrink-wrap and open it. (There has even been talk of the devaluation to a rare book that "eye tracks" can cause. Apparently reading a book leaves tracks. This I did not know.) To these fans, books are a collectible investment. That's fine, but sometimes these collectors lose sight of the fact that a book is meant to be read and that what is most important is what is *inside* a book, not what it is bound in.

King once inscribed the following to one of his biographers in a first edition of his novel, *The Shining*: "Here's a true fact collectors don't seem to know—it's the same story even if you print it on shopping bags..."

To make the transition from shopping bags to e-books, in April 2000, Stephen King released a 16,000-word short story titled "Riding the Bullet" on the Internet. The only place you could get the story was on a bunch of Web sites, including Simon and Schuster's site, plus Amazon's, Barnes & Noble's, and many other e-tailers who served as distributors for the story. The story cost $2.50 (although Amazon and Barnes & Noble gave it away for free for several days) and it was in a format that prevented it from being printed (although this feature was cracked within hours of the story's release and many purchasers did ultimately print it out).

There was no mistake to be made about what "Riding the Bullet" was: This story was intended to be read on a computer or some other type of hand-held electronic "reader." "Riding the Bullet" was a textbook launching of an e-text.

Reportedly, close to 500,000 copies of "Riding the Bullet" were down loaded within the first few days of its availability. King said that he earned around $450,000 for the story, compared with around the $10,000 he would have received if he had published it in *The New Yorker.* The magazine probably would have eagerly accepted this tale for publication…that is if King had offered it to them.

Even though the story sold like crazy and many people wanted to read it, there was some backlash against King and Simon and Schuster for e-publishing it. The story was not available in an alternate print form and it was not possible for purchasers to print it out. (King later announced that the story would be included in a forthcoming short story collection. Initially, the belief was that if you did not have a computer and access to the Internet, you were out of luck.) There was also some negative response to the whole idea of this "book" not actually being a book but instead digital text that had to be read on a screen.

Granted, "Riding the Bullet" was not a book (*novella* is more accurate), but the aforementioned principle of "form vs. function" still applies. The people who were fixated on *how* they had to read the story were completely overlooking *what* they would be able to read: a thrilling Stephen King ghost story that was scary, entertaining, and incredibly well-written.

King was right: "it's *the same story* even if you print it on shopping bags," or computer screens, for that matter.

The Magazine Article

*I**nstant Expert* is intended to help you do the research needed to write a book, magazine article, speech, or term paper; the assumption being that you already have the assignment, and that you need guidance to help you find what you need to know in a timely manner so you can meet your deadline.

For purposes of this book, you have successfully pitched an idea for an article to *Passion for the Past* magazine titled: "In His Own Right: Robert Todd Lincoln." You scored the assignment, and now you have a due date, a required word count, and an agreed-upon fee.

But to back up a couple of blocks before we hit the highway, let's talk for a moment about how you got the assignment in the first place.

Let's assume you have always been a Lincoln buff and have collected many books and articles about Lincoln. You come up with the idea to try and sell an article about Lincoln's oldest son during your reading of the Lincoln materials, by reading *Passion for the Past* magazine, *and* studying the magazine's profile in the latest edition of *Writer's Market.* "Lincolnania always wanted," the blurb said. You knew your idea was a natural for *Passion for the Past*.

John Wood, editor of *Modern Maturity* magazine, in an article written especially for *Writer's Market,* stated, "Professional writers choose ideas that interest them. Beginning writers ask, 'Whatcha got?' There's a big difference."

Indeed there is. And the biggest difference is that the writers who come up with book ideas and magazine article ideas often have a grounding in the subject to begin with. This, of course, does not obviate the need for research, but it does imbue their work with a passion and a liveliness often lacking in works taken on simply for the money or the prestige or as a favor (as is sometimes the case with speeches for groups or organizations. These can be deadly boring because the speaker writes the speech without the aforementioned passion for the subject).

There are many excellent books and articles on how to secure an assignment from a magazine. *Writer's Digest* magazine is a must; as is their annual publication, *Writer's Market.*

In this age of the Internet, there are also e-mailed newsletters for writers on a wide range of topics—ranging from romance short stories to business profiles and horror tales. I myself subscribe to a free e-newsletter called *Dark Echo* (*darkecho@aol.com*), edited by the tireless Paula Guran. I receive *Dark Echo* as an e-mail once a week and it includes up-to-the-minute news about the horror genre—including books, magazines, screenplays, movies, and more. Each issue also includes a current "market watch" feature, in which magazines actively look for stories and articles, along with pay rates, submission procedures, and other relevant information.

The point is, if you have an article idea, there are hungry publications out there always looking for good material. Learn how to submit an article query (again, *Writer's Digest* and *Writer's Market* are invaluable) and target your pitches to the appropriate publications. Remember when we went through the process of categorizing our book by asking ourselves what department of the bookstore our book belonged in? Well, just as publishers target specific audiences, so do magazines (even more so, in fact). You would not pitch an idea about how to keep your car running smoothly to a culinary magazine, right? Research the market and target the appropriate magazines and you will immensely improve your odds of making a sale.

Now let's talk about applying the Six Step System to the writing of your contracted magazine article. By their comparatively brief nature, magazine articles do not require the enormous amount of research that books often do. However, with magazine articles, it is the *right* research with which you need to be concerned.

For your Robert Todd Lincoln article, you will have read the relevant sections of Lincoln biographies, visited the Web sites devoted to Robert, and tracked down and read the articles published about Robert over the years, until you have a body of notes that would allow you to construct your working table of contents. This would be followed by the Chapter by Chapter step (which, in the case of magazine articles, refers to individual sections of the article instead of actual chapters).

JonBenet, Inc.

The magazine article has a limited focus, a book is expansive; the magazine article is fast, a book is leisurely; the magazine article is brief, a book is long. These form, function, and marketplace parameters mandate how the magazine article must be written.

Thus, as an exercise, we will now completely deconstruct a current magazine article. As we do, we will construct a table of contents for the piece, even though it is already written, to illustrate the application of the techniques involved in crafting an article.

The piece we will look at is an article from the February 2000 issue of *Brill's Content* titled "JonBenet, Inc." by Katherine Rosman. (You can read it on the Internet. Surf over to the following URL to take a look: *www.brillscontent.com/features/benet_0200.html.*)

This article runs approximately 8,500 words, which includes two sidebars totaling approximately 700 words. Consistent with the editorial mission statement of *Brill's Content*, the article does not attempt to solve the murder of JonBenet Ramsey. Instead, it looks at how the media has covered the story, who has cashed in on the opportunity, and what it all means after the era of O.J. and Monica Lewinsky.

"JonBenet, Inc." is a "think" piece, meaning that it discusses what events and the responses to those events mean. The author doesn't just tacitly report upon the news—she is critical on her topic, basically asserting that there was never any news to report. Nonetheless, it required research, interviews, and a coherent structure, as much as any article detailing the newest safety features of airplanes...or the life of Robert Todd Lincoln.

Author Katherine Rosman sets the stage for the premise of her article in the opening blurb. In it, she describes the frenzy surrounding the unsolved murder of 6-year-old JonBenet Ramsey: "Lots of local media cashing in on the ravenous appetite of national news outlets for a story that had only one problem: There was never any real news." The subtitle of the piece reinforces her thesis: "Books. Movies. TV. Careers."

First we will discuss the article in detail, and then we will construct a "table of contents" for the piece, working backwards, to show how the piece was put together through research and writing. After a careful reading of the piece, we can identify the Immersion research Rosman did for the article. Her research involved interviewing many people involved in the story, reading a mountain of media stories about the murder, and doing research into the movies, books, and other media coverage of the story. She also viewed documentaries, news footage, and Web sites related to the story.

Rosman quotes more than two dozen people in the piece and maintains her objectivity throughout, never passing judgment on either the Ramseys or the people covering the story. Instead, she simply reports the facts, letting those facts (and the principal players' words) speak for themselves.

The introductory section of the article sets the stage for what is to follow. In the article's opening segment, an actor playing a reporter in a TV movie about the JonBenet murder waits outside a courthouse for a possible real-world jury indictment against JonBenet's parents that never comes. This is followed by FBI statistics on the murders of children, leading smoothly to background facts and statistics about the JonBenet murder.

The author then provides facts about media stories about the murder. She cites the number of stories (438 to date), lists the TV shows that covered the murder (*20/20, 48 Hours, Extra,* among others), mentions newspapers and magazines that have done likewise, and cites a Web site, Joshua-7 (*www.joshua-7.com*) that functions as a tabloid archive. (I jotted down the name of this site for possible use for another project. This is the kind of "noticing" that can be extremely useful for nonfiction writers.)

At this point in the piece, the author quotes JonBenet's father, John Ramsey, who expresses shock at the media coverage of his daughter's murder. To counter this attack, the author then quotes an NBC reporter who defends covering the story. And to add even more balance to her coverage, the author then cites the editor of a Denver newspaper who rejects the NBC reporter's arguments.

Setting the stage for the next section of the article, the author then includes remarks from a Colorado newspaper man named Charlie Brennan who admits that the murder was a golden opportunity for him to make a name for himself. The article then moves into its first titled section: "Footprints in *What* Snow?" Charlie Brennan talks about how he first got involved in covering the story and Rosman reproduces an excerpt from Brennan's original four-page report about the murder, the story in which he revealed his "no footprints in the snow" (outside the Ramsey's house) scoop. The story made national news and Brennan found himself sought after by media all over the country.

The author then discusses how two writers named Daniel Glick and Sherry Keene-Osborn did the research that disproved the "no footprints" story…and how no one in the media picked up on this important development.

After explaining this turn of events, the author then allows Brennan to defend himself. He is quoted as saying that all he did was report what the police said. This leads to his contention that the police were already looking to the parents as the main suspects.

The author then comments that over a period, "For many reporters, getting the story out ultimately became more important than getting it right." She follows that by introducing Jeff Shapiro, a reporter for the tabloid *The Globe*, who alleges that *The Globe* fabricated JonBenet stories to sell papers. The author follows this with a profile of Shapiro in which he justifies going undercover to get a scoop.

Details are then provided about a story alleging that John Ramsey had given his pilot, Michael Archuleta, a box of damning evidence. The story was ultimately proven to be inaccurate but Shapiro became a celebrity from covering the story and ultimately got a job with *Time* magazine. To balance her reporting, Rosman presents allegations by a homicide detective interviewed by Shapiro who claims that Shapiro distorted his comments. The author follows up on this allegation by querying *Time* magazine about the charges against Shapiro. *Time* tells Rosman that they had no problem with the piece penned by Shapiro because the homicide detective had not complained to the magazine.

The article then continues with its second titled section (considerably shorter than the first section), called "The Ramseys Are Fair Game."

This section begins with the story of freelance photographer Frank Coffman taking a picture of John Ramsey and Ramsey attacking him. (The author derived the title of this section from a direct quote by Coffman in which he stated that felt that the Ramseys were "fair game.") The author goes on to relate how once word got out that Coffman had pictures, even *The New York Times* called wanting to buy them. Coffman admits to the author that he also took pictures of the inside of the Ramsey house and sold them to a movie production company. The author sums up this section with this: "That the *Times* considers it newsworthy that a 'stalkerazzi' photographer claims to have had his collar grabbed by John Ramsey indicates how far even the most legitimate of news outlets have gone for a JonBenet story."

The third section, "Getting In on the Action," tells the story of radio talk show host Peter Boyles whose ratings have skyrocketed since he began voicing his JonBenet opinions every morning. The author recounts the story of when Boyles ran an open letter to the Ramseys in several newspapers accusing them of being the murderers. (This was after the Ramseys ran an ad asking for help in finding their daughter's murderer.) This stunt got Boyles on *Dateline NBC*, *Rivera Live*, and *Good Morning, America*. The author also reveals that Boyles co-produced a CD of JonBenet parody songs, including a song called "Big Bad John." What some have decried as profiteering on Boyles's part is not commented on editorially by the author. Instead, she remains impartial and presents the facts for the readers to make up their own minds.

This section—after the first mention of what the author calls the "Lynch the Ramseys Brigade" — moves into a discussion of TV journalist Geraldo Rivera's mock trial of the Ramseys. The panel gives JonBenet's parents a guilty verdict, along with the audience's screams of approval. She concludes the section by disclosing that Rivera was later given a $30 million, six-year contract by NBC.

The fourth section, "All the News That's Leaked Into Print," begins with a profile of newspaper columnist Chuck Green, who has written 80 "JonBenet" columns so far and believes the Ramseys are guilty. The author discusses how journalists covered the JonBenet story by reporting the spin that was deliberately leaked to them by sources, and quotes Green as saying, "That's how journalism works." Rosman also touches on how leaks emerge from "tight-lipped" sources. This is followed by a comment from a journalism professor who claims that law enforcement agencies used Green to test JonBenet theories and to print what they wanted to see printed, followed by comments from a radio personality who claims to have had leaks fed to her for dissemination. This section concludes with a discussion of how there are now two journalistic camps in the JonBenet field: The Ramseys are "guilty" or they are "not guilty" and it depends on who talks to whom. The author illustrates this point by mentioning a British documentary that defended the Ramseys being denounced by Ramsey critics, while those in the "not guilty" camp defended the documentary.

The fifth and final section of the article is titled "The Ramseys Take a Turn" and reveals that the Ramseys sold their story to a Christian publisher. (This article was published before the Ramsey's memoir hit the stores.) The author discusses the media attention to the Ramseys after the grand jury decided not to indict them, and poses the question: Are the Ramseys profiteering and attempting to cash in on their daughter's murder? Their answer to this question is provided by the Ramseys's attorney who says the parents are not cashing in. He explains that defending themselves has cost them a great deal of money and that any proceeds from the book will go towards paying off those debts. Any profits above that will go to charity. The article concludes with John Ramsey blasting the media for accusing them of cashing in on their daughter's murder. The article's last line is a quote from John Ramsey: "There's so much hypocrisy."

•••

Now that we have reviewed this well-written and balanced piece, let's construct the article's "table of contents" as the author might have done before she began actually writing it. Here is what the table of contents to "JonBenet, Inc." by Katherine Rosman might look like:

Introduction

- Courthouse/TV movie scene.
- FBI stats.
- JonBenet background details.
  - media coverage specifics.
- John Ramsey "shock" quote.
- NBC reporter (pro-coverage).
- Denver editor (anti-coverage).
- Introduce Charlie Brennan.

Part 1: "Footprints in *What* Snow?"

- Charlie Brennan's initiation into the story.
  - The "no footprints" scoop.
  - Excerpt from original Brennan report.
- Glick and Keene-Osborn—story is false.
- Media drops the ball.
- Brennan defends himself.
- Introduce Jeff Shapiro.
- *The Globe's* fabricated stories.
- Profile Shapiro.
- Did John Ramsey give his pilot the evidence against him?
- Shapiro & *Time* magazine.

Part 2: "The Ramseys Are Fair Game"

- Frank Coffman takes a picture; John Ramsey attacks.
- *The New York Times* calls.
- Coffman "fair game" quote.

Part 3: "Getting In on the Action"

- Peter Boyle's radio ratings.
- Peter Boyle's open letter to the Ramseys.
- Peter Boyle on TV.
- Peter Boyle's CD.

• Geraldo Rivera's mock trial of the Ramseys.
• Geraldo scores with NBC.

Part 4: "All the News That's Leaked Into Print"
• Profile of Chuck Green.
• The mechanism of journalistic leaks.
• The two JonBenet camps.
• The "not guilty" British documentary.

Part 5: "The Ramseys Take a Turn"
• The Ramseys write a book.
• The grand jury does not indict.
• Are the Ramseys profiteering?
• The Ramseys' lawyer speaks.
• "There's so much hypocrisy."

Sidebars (by Katherine Rosman):
• The TV movie.
• The documentary.

Sidebars (by staff of *Brill's Content*):
• The books.
• The Santa scavengers.
• The Web sites.

If Rosman's article did not exist, this table of contents would probably have guided her through the writing of "JonBenet, Inc." and resulted in a piece that probably would have looked like what she ultimately ended up publishing.

The point of all this is that the working table of contents can be written until you have a piece that has a beginning, a middle, and an end. It can then be polished, revised, tweaked, and buffed up as needed. The heart of the article is there and from that point, it's all cosmetic surgery.

The magazine article is an extremely flexible art form—and there are thousands of magazines looking for material on a regular basis. If you get an assignment, approach the writing of the piece in a smooth, structured manner and your end results should be what you (and your readers) will consider a pleasure to read. And that's why we buy the magazines in the first place, right?

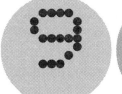

chapter

The Speech

The first speech I ever gave was to a group of Rotary Club members at one of their weekly lunch meetings shortly after my first book came out.

This is how the Rotary Club meetings work: Each week a different Rotarian (as they like to be called) brings a guest speaker to their midday meeting. The speaker gets lunch (usually a meal that could more accurately be described as a dinner), but no honorarium or stipend. The speakers range from the local chiropractor or veterinarian to the head of a veterans' group or a high school principal. The guest speakers talk about their area of specialty and the speeches usually last between 20 and 30 minutes. The inclusion of talks at the weekly meetings is meant to encourage local involvement and participation in many different issues and to allow area businesspeople and members of the community to get to know each other.

I was invited by a friend who owned a clothing store a few doors down from where I was working at the time. Back then I was still managing a family jewelry store full-time. I knew

many neighboring businessmen and my recent book sale had become local news of some import. This would be a good way, I thought, of promoting the book and getting some local press. Also, many Rotary Club meetings are taped by local public access cable television and rebroadcast endlessly—and I knew that couldn't hurt either. I would not be allowed to sell books at the luncheon but I could hand out flyers or bookmarks if I wanted to.

For three weeks, I prepared (overprepared is the better word) for this speech. I was thinking...well, I don't know *what* I was thinking—perhaps that warring nations would lay down their weapons or that the ozone layer would heal itself after I uttered my deathless words. Or not.

The day of my first speech (I was actually referring to it in my mind as My First Speech, in caps) I dressed to the nines and packed my briefcase with copies of my book, a dozen (maybe more) note cards, some *Andy Griffith Show* cast photos from my book, copies of my biography, breath mints, and enough pens to rewrite my entire book. It would be an understatement to say I was a little nervous.

This was, after all, My First Speech and I had no idea if I would be able to deliver the goods. I had heard all about bombing on stage, about flop sweat, about comics coming up with bad one-liners in order to minimize the effect of getting a dead response from their audience. Every nightmare that could occur in front of a crowd went through my mind.

When I arrived, I was greeted warmly and thanked profusely for taking time out of my schedule to speak to the Rotary Club. These may be platitudes, but I sensed that my welcome was sincere and genuine. The president of the club personally took me around to almost every member and introduced me with grace and flattery. By the time the salad came I felt like a bigshot!

At Rotary meetings, before the guest speaker is brought on, they go through business, which usually involves a discussion of things on the agenda (such as charity food drives, scheduling confirmations, status of ill members, and other miscellaneous matters.) Oh, and they sing too. Yeah. Lord help us all.

Every member rises from his seat and the whole group sings a song in unison. The day I spoke they sang, I think, "God Bless America," although it could have been "The Star-Spangled Banner" for all I know. It was nevertheless (and always is) something patriotic.

And then it was my turn. (To speak, not to sing.) I was introduced, the Rotarians applauded, and I was off to the races.

All in all, it went very well for My First Speech. I spoke about how I had spent seven years writing proposals and submitting book ideas to publishers before selling my first book. I also spoke about the dozens of rejections I received before placing *Mayberry, My Home Town* with a publisher.

My philosophy then—and now—is to never take no for an answer. Because I had sensed immediately that the themes of personal initiative, self-determination, commitment, courageous optimism, and self-confidence would play well with this crowd, I scrapped my planned lecture. Instead, I talked openly about my feelings on receiving six rejection letters on the same day. I talked about what it took to forge ahead with confidence, knowing that my book was a good one. I knew that the day would come when I would find the right publisher, the one who would recognize that there was an audience for the book I wanted to write…and that I was the guy to write it.

I also talked about writing as a full-time business, how writers got paid every six months, and how to plan accordingly. This especially struck a chord with men who understood what it took to start and grow a successful business.

My decision (based solely on my intuitive reading of the crowd) proved to be right. My speech went over *huge* with the Rotarians, every one of whom was a self-made success.

Remember, this isn't story hour; don't read to your audience!

The whole point of this is that the biggest mistake someone can make in giving a speech is to refuse to adapt to the tenor of the audience. I know that many speakers write out their speeches and then deliver them verbatim. This comes across poorly. Think about someone standing behind a podium, reading a paper to you. Have you ever sat in an audience where you've been read to? It can be sleep-inducing. This approach completely eliminates the possibility of personal interaction between you, the speaker, and your listeners.

Interesting enough, I recently saw the former Mrs. Billy Joel, supermodel Christie Brinkley, giving a speech about the danger of nuclear reactors. Christie read her text word for word off pages lying in front of her. Now, if anyone is going to hold my attention, it's Christie Brinkley. But the truth is that even a supermodel can come across as dull when *reading* a speech instead of speaking extemporaneously (no matter how planned out the extemporaneous remarks actually are). Christie gave it the old college try and did try to sell the speech with a somewhat impassioned delivery. But her constant need to look down to read the next sentence before uttering it was distracting and left me with a "ho hum" reaction to her message.

Also worth considering is that, if you *know* that the complete text of your speech is laid out in front of you, you may not prepare as thoroughly as you might if you have to deliver a talk with nothing but a few note cards to cue you through the speech. A written text is a safety net that often results in a dull, dry, flatly-presented speech lacking all spontaneity whatsoever. These are the kinds of speeches people either do not remember, walk out of, sit through, or later tear to shreds because it was "a waste of time."

So the main rule in giving a speech is to not overprepare. Do not write an essay that you plan to read before a crowd. Giving a speech is not a recitation. Giving a speech is talking *to* people, not *at* people. It is, by its very nature, *interactive*. An essay is meant to be read and is insular and contemplative. Mixing the two is an unstable concoction.

Keep "expert notes"

I am not saying to simply stand up and start talking without cue cards, notes, or any other materials. That could be a disaster. You could get off to a good start but then get distracted and lose your place. You will then tend to forget certain points you wanted to make. (Besides, using the word "uh" too often is far from wise.)

I usually get 5 x 7 index cards, write my notes on them, and highlight key elements of the speech. These are extremely useful in keeping me on track. Often, a glance down at a card filled with key words is enough to keep me focused, yet still allows me to maintain eye contact with the audience.

With thanks to David Letterman...

One of my most popular speeches is my talk titled "The Italian Top Ten: The Ten Most Influential Italians in World History."

This speech is based on my book *The Italian 100: A Ranking of the Most Influential Political, Cultural, and Scientific Figures, Past and Present.* For purposes of my spin-off speech, I put together brief talks on the top 10 figures in my book. For entertainment value, I present them the way David Letterman does his Top 10 list: backwards, from number 10 to number 1.

> **There's nothing that puts the audience to sleep faster than an author reading his nonfiction prose. Yes, she/he can illustrate her/his talk with a few well-chosen paragraphs, but if you read five pages, expect snores."**
>
> **—Carla Cohen, Politics & Prose Books**

My Italian Top 10 are:

10. Leonardo Da Vinci
9. Michelangelo
8. Filippo Mazzei
7. Evangelista Torricelli
6. Leonardo Fibonacci
5. Alessandro Volta
4. Enrico Fermi
3. Guglielmo Marconi
2. Christopher Columbus
1. Galileo Galilei

For my talk, I put together two important compilations of information to bring with me: First, I printed out the first 10 chapters from my book and put them in a three-ring binder in reverse order, from Chapter 10 to Chapter 1.

I put a colored tab on the first page of each chapter and labeled the tab with the Italian figure's name.

Then, I went through each chapter and highlighted all the key passages, important points, or notable quotations.

This blue binder is my backup resource and my safety net. If I find myself floundering for information while on stage, or if my notes are not triggering the flow of words I need to talk about each Italian notable authoritatively, I always have the complete text from my book to fall back on.

My second "helper"—and this is the most important one—is the aforementioned stack of 10 5" x 7" index cards, one for each of the personalities I talk about. On the front of each of these cards are bulleted talking points. These are key words and phrases that start me off, allowing me to explicate and elaborate verbally...making it look as if I speak off the top of my head.

And that is critical: An important point to remember is that I know the material I lecture on backwards and forwards. That is my strength, and it should be every speaker's strength. If you are to give a speech, you should know the material well enough for it flow from you completely naturally. You should not use the opportunity of a public speech to *learn* the material and refine your thoughts about the subject "live," so to speak.

Your aids should be nothing more than that: helpers, not the speech itself. When you are driving a route that you have driven a thousand times, you rarely glance at the street signs or highway exit signs, right? They're there, but you already know the way. If the signs weren't there, you'd still get to where you were going.

Lecture aids are like those street signs. They are there to glance at to reinforce that you are headed in the right direction. However, you should know the material well enough so that you could deliver the speech without them if need be.

To show you how I keep on the right path, here is a look at two of my Italian Top 10 cue cards. (These are direct transcripts of my cards.)

I always place these cards in front of me at the podium and, to lessen the possibility of getting lost during my talk, I also highlight key words and

Sample index card

> **GUGLIELMO MARCONI (1874-1937) b. 4/25/1874 (3)**
> **Italian father/Irish mother—Bologna**
>
> - invented wireless communication
> - d. 7/20/1937 (67) all radio station in world broadcast 2 mins. silence
> - paved way for invention of TV
> - "What big ears he has!"
> - "With these ears he'll be able to hear the still small voice of the air" [mother]
> - 1895—age 21—produced 1st working radio device
> - Marconi offered wireless to Italian govt.—they passed
> - 11/1896—Marconi's Wireless Telegraph Company Ltd.
> - 1899—1st wireless message across English Channel
> - Thursday—12/12/1901—radio message—"S"—fr. England to Newfoundland—this marked invention of radio
> - 1906—1st voice transmission via radio waves
> - 1910—successfully sent radio message fr. Ireland to Argentina—6,000 miles
> - 1909—won Nobel Prize Physics for invention of radio
> - Hart—"telephone" [read quote]

important dates in yellow on the index cards. These cards and their key words allow me to depend on my personality and my base of knowledge when giving a speech, a mandate that always results in a much more natural, and thus much more appealing and interesting, presentation.

"But he has a great personality..."

And that brings us to *your* personality when you are on stage. Have one. Project your personality when you are speaking. You want people to walk out of that room enlightened by your words. But you also want them

Sample index card

FILIPPO MAZZEI (1730-1816) b. 12/25/1730 (8)
Poggio

- responsible for "all men are created equal" in Dec. of Ind.
- studied medicine in Florence—practiced in Turkey until 25
- moved to London—imprtng co.—olive oil/cheese/wine— over 20 yrs
- 1770—met Ben Franklin -BF persuaded him to move to US to do agrcltrl exprmnts in Virginia
- 1773—sailed to America w/ tailor & vine cuttings
- est. farm in Vrgnia—next door to Thomas Jefferson
- began writing essays for Vrgnia Gzzte—"Furioso"—Jffrsn translated into English fr. Italian
- "All men are by nature..." [read excerpt fr. chapter]
- Jffrsn used FM's words verbatim in Vrgnia Constitution's Bill of Rights
- 1776—changed words to "All men are created equal" for D of I
- 1779—trvld to Italy to borrow money to help US cause— Franklin persuaded him not to—only the country should borrow
- 1786 (56) returned to Europe—wrote 4-volume history of 13 colonies
- died in Pisa 3/19/1816 at 85
- honored by FDR in 1941
- 1980—postage stamp—250th annvrsry his birth

---

thinking that you were a funny, engaging, charming person...someone they wouldn't mind knowing in real life.

Here are two secrets to effective public speaking. (And I know the one about imagining everyone in the audience sitting there in their underwear, but that seems to be most effective for calming down a nervous speaker.)

Instead of seeing people in their skivvies, these two secrets to effective public speaking may prove to be more effective:

1. Speak as though you are talking to every person in the audience individually.
2. Speak as though you have personally known every person in the audience for years.

These two tips work…in a big way. You will find that people will make steady and repeated eye contact with you, and that they will actually begin to respond to you personally as you speak. Their faces will change the way people's do when you are having a one-on-one conversation with them. Many in the crowd will acquire that "lost in the moment" expression on their face as they continue to respond to their sense that you are speaking only to each of them.

The Zen of a speech:
Begin without beginning

An important part of every speech is the opening. I always try to do what I call a "cold start." Rather then beginning with a general introduction and a summary of the topic I am going to talk about, I recount an interesting fact or anecdote about my subject. You will notice that the best speakers often begin speaking as though you caught them in the middle of a conversation. This is very effective and instantly grabs the audience's attention.

For instance, for my Italian Top 10 talk, as soon as I walked on stage after being introduced, I immediately said,

I have a friend in Georgia…Dave…who's not even 10 percent Italian. In fact, I think he's mostly German and English. When we became friends I tried to turn him on to some Italian delicacies. One day, I described a white broccoli pizza to him, which the Italians in the audience probably know is chopped broccoli sauteed in oil and garlic and used as a topping on a pizza. There's no tomato sauce and that's why it's called a "white broccoli" pie. After I mentioned this incredible pizza to Dave, he got this confused look on his face and then he said, "White broccoli? Isn't that cauliflower?" I then explained the difference and silently thanked St. Anthony that I had been born of Italian parents.

This story always gets a laugh and it always gets my presentation off to a good start. You'll notice that even though I say the above passage almost verbatim, it reads as very conversational, very informal. This is deliberate. After giving a few speeches on the same subject, you will find that you will be able to say the same things over and over, but with a genuinely natural tone and presentation.

Actors do this automatically. Even though they are reciting written words, there is a usually a spontaneity and a dollop of improvisation in their performance. I have read along in a script as I watched the movie made from it many times, and no matter how finely crafted the dialogue (as in the scripts of Woody Allen, Oliver Stone, or David Mamet, for instance), the actors *always* make changes in the way they say their lines. They say that the words have to "feel right" in their mouths before they can say them with conviction and with a natural style. Once, I interviewed a famous director who told me that one of the most important talents an actor can possess is the ability to do a line-reading naturally—as though they were the actual character speaking in his or her daily life.

This is also applicable in giving a speech. Again, if you talk to each person individually, you will come across as open, warm and, above all, natural.

To elaborate on this, here is what I might open with as my "cold start" for our aforementioned hypothetical Lincoln speech, "Father Abe: Parenting Tips of Abraham Lincoln":

Tad Lincoln, Mary and Abe's youngest boy, was a handful when he was a child. If he lived today, his parents would probably have put him on Ritalin. Back then, though, his rowdy ways were accepted by his father as part of his personality—even when he ran through a formal party at the Lincolns' house swinging a large ham. Abe would laugh things like this off; his guests cleared out of the way and tried to avoid the little Lincoln. Today we're going to talk about...

Again, this is a conversational anecdote that sets a tone and instantly engages the audience. Immediately, questions will be running through the minds of the audience members: Did Abraham Lincoln really allow one of his sons to run wild? Were Lincoln's sons spoiled brats? Where was the mother when all this was going on? And the fact that they will be wondering about these things will make them very receptive to what you are going to say—as long as you know what you are talking about and you answer the questions the audience wants answered. If you present facts that lead to questions in the audience's mind and then do not answer these questions, you will inevitably be asked them during the often obligatory question and answer period that follows your speech.

The Q & A

And that brings us to a discussion of the Q & A. Many speeches will conclude with a question and answer period—the Q & A.

Ideally, you will have covered your material well enough so that the questions you receive allow you to expand on your material, rather than providing essay-type answers to difficult questions you are not prepared to cover. All that aside, though, here are some tips for this period of interchange between you and your audience.

When you first open up the floor to questions, allow a little time for people to raise their hands. Sometimes, when you say, "Are there any questions?" no one will make a move. It might be that no one wants to be the first (like in elementary school, remember?). Nine times out of 10, someone *will* eventually raise a hand (bless them) and ask you a question about the subject you just spoke about.

Listen to the question carefully and then—this is important—repeat the question for the audience, even if the room is small and everyone heard it. Then answer the question as completely as possible and address your answer to the person who asked the question.

Gauge the scope of your responses by the number of hands raised and the time allotted for the Q & A. If it doesn't look like there will be too many questions, you can let your answers run long. If there are a dozen or more hands in the air, keep your answers brief.

As you near the end of the time allocated, announce when you will take one more question. You may have seen this done at the White House briefing room's press conferences and elsewhere and what it does is serve to wrap things up. When you call on someone, you could say, "Okay, you in the blue shirt and then one more after this." Then after you answer Mr. Blue Shirt's question, say, "Okay, last question."

Con te partiro (Time to say goodbye)

When your time in the spotlight has come to an end, I have found it a nice touch to "clap back" at the audience.

When everyone is clapping for you, briefly extend your arms and clap as though you are clapping for them. This is usually seen as a very warm gesture of appreciation and thanks and is kind of charming. This doesn't work all the time (especially if the applause for you is, well, sparse). But if you have scored with your audience and the applause seems to be heartfelt, thanking them in this way is a unique way of reciprocating for their attention.

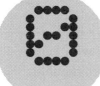
The Term Paper

> **Most of the arguments to which I am a party fall somewhat short of being impressive, owing to the fact that neither I nor my opponent knows what we are talking about.**
>
> —**Robert Benchley**

efore I begin, allow me to respond to Robert Benchley's witty bon mot cited above. I can do it in six words: *Know what you are talking about.*

In the hypothetical research and writing scenario I have set before you, you have received instructor approval for a term paper titled, "Robert Todd Lincoln: The Price of Having a Presidential Father."

As I discussed in Chapter 13, your paper must be no less than 10 pages in length, consist of 2,500 to 3,000 words, and be in proper form, complete with footnotes and a bibliography. So where do you begin?

Because you already have your title, you know the subject areas you will need to research. You are to look at Abraham Lincoln, specifically his life and times; his wife, Mary Todd, and her behavior as a mother; and most importantly, the life of their oldest boy Robert, and how being the son of Abraham Lincoln affected his life path.

Immersion

Using my six step system, you begin with Immersion. You hit the Internet, the library, and the bookstores. You assemble the body of materials you will read and review to find the facts you need to write your paper.

You should skim and spot-read your materials quickly to get an idea as to which books, articles, and other materials will be of value for your paper. Then you can follow the Six Step System and read through the materials more carefully, highlighting, underlining, and making notes, until you have a strong base of source information.

Your thesis statement

What is different about a term paper (as compared to a book, article, or speech, all of which are created from "whole cloth," so to speak) is that you must begin your paper with a well-defined thesis. The thesis is the point you plan to expound upon and ultimately prove in your text.

For our theoretical paper, your thesis can be discerned by asking the question, "What is the price of having a presidential father?" As a response to this question, you have determined (as we discussed in Chapter 13) that your thesis is the following:

Having a presidential father does not automatically translate into lifelong benefits. Sometimes, being the offspring of a president can be a detriment to living a fulfilling life because the child is often perceived as standing in the shadow of his father and his accomplishments are often compared with his father's.

From this jumping-off point, you then write your thesis statement. This tells your reader what your paper is about. A possible thesis statement for your paper might be the following:

A commonly held belief is that being the son of a President is a *prize*. Many Americans would dismiss the notion that, instead, having a president as a father carries a *price*.

In this paper, I will attempt to prove that being the offspring of a president can sometimes be a detriment to living a fulfilling life. Why? Because the White House child is often perceived as standing in the shadow of his or her father, and many people—family, friends, the American public—reflexively (and unfairly) compare his or her accomplishments with those of their father, the president.

Robert Todd Lincoln, the subject of this paper, was the eldest son of Abraham Lincoln, and his life was profoundly affected by the legacy of his martyred, iconic father and the related historical events Robert lived through. These facts lead naturally to the question, "Would Robert Todd Lincoln's life been any different if he was not Lincoln's son and if his father had not been assassinated?"

Your paper's structure

Term papers have a specific structure. Here is a streamlined outline applicable for most college-level term papers:

Introduction
- Show how the thesis was derived from a question needing to be answered.
- Form a hypothesis that addresses the issue.
- State your thesis.

The body
- Prove your thesis.
- Begin each paragraph with a topic sentence, stating what you will discuss in the paragraph.
- Buttress your argument with citations from primary and secondary sources.

Conclusion
- Sum up your findings and restate your conclusions.
- Provide a properly constructed bibliography, listing all the sources you cited in your paper.

The Six Step System works quite nicely with this outline. In fact, the only changes you would need to make in the system would be to consider your term paper outline the working table of contents and the writing of the individual sections of the paper the completion of the Chapter by Chapter step. It all fits together rather neatly, wouldn't you say?

As for format, most term papers are double-spaced, with single-spaced footnotes on the bottom of the page, along with the bibliography at the end of the paper. Footnotes on each page are still used and are often acceptable, but standard format in academia today is to use endnotes.

For our Robert Todd Lincoln paper, I think I would probably use the John Goff biography, *Robert Todd Lincoln: A Man In His Own Right* as my primary source as well as the Ruth Randall biography, *Lincoln's Sons*. Additional sources I would study carefully would include one or more bios of Mary Todd Lincoln, Web site articles about Robert's brothers, and newspaper articles from the period in which Robert is quoted directly. I would also review the better Lincoln biographies (Sandburg's, Donald's, among others) for information about Robert's upbringing and interaction with his three brothers, as well as with his parents.

Your writer's voice in your term paper

As for technique and style, my advice would be to tone down your use of informal language. But, on the other hand, do not effect a phony academic or pedantic tone. And never try and mimic the narrative voice of the writers you are reading as part of your research. Professors and instructors can smell artifice like the garbage it is. Your teachers can easily sense when you are BS-ing. So instead, do the research and write your paper from a base of knowledge. Your writer's voice will reflect your understanding of your subject. You may get a bad grade anyway (misspelled words, a faulty argument, a lack of documentation, a ridiculous thesis, among others). But at least you won't have to worry about plagiarism charges (or being laughed at by misusing words such as "opprobrious" [shameful] or "sesquipedalian" [a long word]).

A (plus), B (minus), C (O.D.)...

That brings us to a discussion of "paper mills." Paper mills are companies that will sell you a term paper written to order, or one from a catalog listing thousands of papers covering hundreds of subjects. Today, term papers are available for a price on the Internet.

Some paper mills are very specific about what they are providing: research and writing services, not complete term papers for a student to submit in lieu of doing his or her own work. In fact, one company I contacted includes a disclaimer on their order form declaring that "the research material purchased...is intended for and will be used for research purposes only." Yeah, right.

That disclaimer is probably something the company's legal department insisted the purchasers sign to protect the company from being charged with helping a student obtain a degree or a good grade. Students buy term papers from these companies and turn them in as their own work. This is fraud, and you should *never* do it.

However, believe it or not, these "research and writing services" companies can actually assist you in your own research. (This is all the companies say they're offering to do, after all.)

If I had to actually write our hypothetical term paper, I would have no qualms about ordering relevant term papers from one or more paper mills (if I could afford them, of course—papers run between $6 to $16 per double-spaced page, plus shipping) as part of the Immersion step of the Six Step System.

The papers sold by these companies are written by professional writers and scholars, are impeccably researched, meticulously footnoted, and usually include a comprehensive bibliography. These papers can provide tremendous amounts of quality information. This can not only enhance your understanding of your topic, but also lead you to other sources by referring to the texts cited in the accompanying bibliography.

If you find yourself tempted to do more than just use the paper as a research tool, remember that the whole point of writing a term paper is for *you* to do the research, learn the material, take a stand, and form an opinion about the subject. This is called *learning* and that's what you are going to school for, isn't it? Also keep in mind that if you turn in a bought term paper you bought and your ruse is discovered, you will at the very least, flunk the class, and, at worst, get kicked out of school.

•••

In conclusion, here are some final tips for applying the Six Step System to the writing of a term paper:

- Start early.
- Do more research than you can possibly use.
- Never turn in your first draft.
- Use your computer's spell-checker one time, and one time only, specifically to look for egregious spelling mistakes. Then use *your eyes* to proofread for every subsequent spell-check. (Spell-checking it again, however, never hurts.)
- Make your introduction and conclusion the strongest—and best-written—sections of your paper.
- Do not use slang or informal language.
- Provide a title page formatted according to your professor's instructions.
- Eschew obfuscation.
- Avoid the passive voice, unless it is more appropriate for the sentence in question than the active voice.
- Number your pages in the upper right hand corner. Put the title of the paper and your last name in the upper left hand corner of every page.
- Be sure your punctuation is flawless. If you don't know how to punctuate a particular phrase, clause, sentence, etc., look it up or ask someone.
- Even though a term paper is a scholarly work, be entertaining. Your professor will appreciate the effort.
- Did I mention that you should start early?

section III

First Aid
for Writers

chapter **21**

34 Rules to Write By

> **"** *In the fight between you and the world, back the world.* **"**
>
> —**Frank Zappa**

ome of these rules are harsh. I'm sorry, but the truth is that publishing is not for wimps. Anyone can write, but choosing to try and make a living at writing by publishing regularly in magazines and/or by writing books is extremely difficult. This list is for those of you who fall into this category.

This probably explains why there are so many one-book authors. The adrenaline and euphoria carry these one-hit wonders through the writing, deadline, editing, and publication process of their first efforts. But then their second books transmute into serious work and after all, *There's Something About Mary* is on cable yet again. Oh, and the sock drawer needs to be organized…and what about those dishes…hmm….

This reality also explains why there are fewer than 5,000 writers in the United States making a living by writing. All the others—because there are a thousand books published each week in America—have to supplement their writing income by working another job.

However, this is not always bad, because writing for the art and love of the craft often makes for an inspired work.

Case in point: I was working full-time when I wrote my 750,000-word *Complete Stephen King Encyclopedia.*

I was putting in close to 50 hours a week at a family jewelry business and approximately 30 hours a week researching and writing the *Encyclopedia.* The book took five years of this kind of sustained research and writing, but it resulted in a monumental tome.

The success of that book allowed me to re-tire from the jewelry business and write full-time. But irony of iro-nies, I have not been able to update the *Encyclopedia* (which is now 10 years out of date) because I can't afford to spend five years doing the necessary work now.

> *To get it right, be born with luck or else make it. Never give up. A little money helps, but what really gets it right is to never face the facts."*
>
> **—Ruth Gordon**

Since 1990, I have written and published an average of three books a year, because I am a "mid-list writer." My books sell well and I have a readership, but this does not translate into the kind of income that would allow me to work on anything I damned well please.

You know...Ars gratis artis: "Art for art's sake."

All that aside, in this writer's opinion, the writing and publishing of books is still the single most important mechanism for the communication of ideas, the perpetuation of the human spirit, and the chronicling of the sum and substance of our civilization throughout the world.

But it's a different paradigm when you choose to make writing your career. Then the rules change, and it is my hope that the following suggestions will be helpful for those of you who wish to someday pay your mortgages and buy your daily bread with your words.

Many of these rules apply to those who are already writing for publication. Some are general guidelines for writing as a hobby or as a source of income. And some are just ways to be polite and courteous and professional when working in the world of words. But remember the old Turkish adage: Be careful what you wish for; you may get it.

1. Always reread your pages before printing them out.

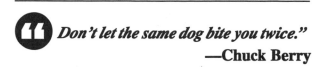

Don't let the same dog bite you twice."
—Chuck Berry

2. Always spell-check your pages before printing them out.

3. Dedicate at least one book to your editor.

4. Do not be surprised if you do a book signing at a local bookstore and you end up sitting there for two hours without signing and selling one book.

5. Do not leave 6-minute-long messages on your editor's voice mail during the night. He or she will probably listen to the first few seconds and then skip to the next message. Voice mail is not the forum for pitching your book or article ideas.

6. Donate one copy of each of your books to your alma mater and your local library.

7. Even if you buy your books online, be sure to visit a major bookstore at least once a month.

8. Everyone in the publishing industry—every bookstore employee, everyone in the media,

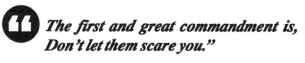

The first and great commandment is, Don't let them scare you."
—Elmer Davis

and almost everyone you know on an intimate basis or as an acquaintance—will not care that you had a book or an article published. Also, there will be people in your immediate family who will never even open your book. (And these are the same people who will expect you to give them a free copy of your book instead of them having to buy it.)

9. Get a post office box.

10. Get to know the librarians at your local library.

11. Have 500 book- marks printed up for each of your books. You can design them on the computer,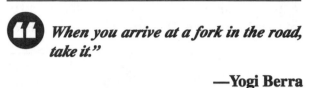

    When you arrive at a fork in the road, take it."

    —Yogi Berra

    and print out camera-ready copy from your laser printer (or make a PDF file). A local printshop can do them in a couple of days at a very reasonable cost. This is an inexpensive way of promoting you and your book. And it offers a way to give something signed to people who attend one of your lectures or book-signings...but do not buy a book. A bookmark keeps your name and the title of your book in front of them for a long time to come. (And they may end up buying a book later.)

12. Have an updated bibliography of your published works handy at all times.

13. Have extra toner and printer paper on hand at all times.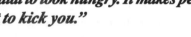

    It is fatal to look hungry. It makes people want to kick you."

    —George Orwell

14. If someone asks you what you're working on and you respond with more than one sentence, you are saying too much. Save it for the page. (The person asking is probably just being polite and doesn't really care to hear a 15-minute exegesis of your latest project when he could be home watching the World Wrestling Foundation.)

    However, feel free to bounce ideas off people whose opinion you consider valuable. For me it's my agent and my editor. For some (like Stephen King) it's his wife and his editor. Other writers talk things out with a fellow writer, teacher, friend, or family member. Pick your sounding boards carefully but do make use of these people. Someone can ask the right question or make the comment that will help you focus or open up narrative opportunities you may not have thought of.

15. If you choose to (or have to) drink decaf, why bother?

16. If you end up writing full-time, do not expect to be able to read for enjoyment anymore. After reading and writing all day long, the last thing you will want to do at the end of the day is pick up a book.

17. If you have a business card made, put your name, mailing address, phone number, fax number, and e-mail address on it. Do not put "Author" or "Writer" under your name, no matter how sorely you are tempted to do so. The exception to this rule is if you are a writer-for-hire who takes on writing assignments (such as corporate writing, speech writing, magazine articles, interviews written to order, and other types of freelance work commissioned for a fee).

18. If you have to mail one of your books to someone, wrapping it twice in thick brown shipping paper is more than adequate and is considerably cheaper to ship (because it's lighter) than packing it in a cardboard box.

19. If you lecture about your book, do not expect anyone in the audience to have read it. And do not expect anyone in the audience to buy it after hearing you speak.

20. I listen to music to block out distractions while I'm writing, and I find that Nirvana, Everclear, Led Zeppelin, *The Last Days of Disco* soundtrack, and anything by Enya make especially good aural masks for me. Also, anything by Mozart, Vivaldi, Philip Glass, Mahler, Handel, or Bach also works very well for the classically-minded. But as in all situations where we need to distract our minds from stimulus in order to focus, one writer's stimulation is another's sedation (and vice versa). Find your bliss and use it.

21. Keep a pad and pencil by your bedside at all times.

22. Meet your deadlines.

23. Never expect to receive a royalty check—be grateful when you do. My advice is to only depend on advances (they're nonrefundable). Royalties are gravy. If you write full-time, it

is extremely dangerous to allow your income to be dependent on the vagaries of book sales.

24. Never respond to a critic. Always respond to your fan mail.

25. You can never have too many sticky notes. Any color is fine, but yellow is the most professional.

26. Read your book contract. Book contracts are potent proof of the power of words. I am referring specifically to what's known as the "cross-collateralization" clause found in almost all book contracts as a standard condition. The essence of this deadly clause is three little words: "or any other." The cross-collateralization clause only applies to you if you do more than one book for a single publisher. But what it states is that if one book earns money for you and another does not, the publisher can apply earnings from the successful book to the advance owed on an unsuccessful book.

   Let's say you sign a book contract and receive a $10,000 advance (known officially as an "advance against royalties"). This means that the first $10,000 your book earns in royalties goes toward paying back your advance. Now let's say that after *Book Number One* hits the stores, you sign a new contract with the same publisher for *Book Number Two* and receive another $10,000 advance. Fast forward a year. The first book bombed; the second did well. *Book Number One* earned no royalties and did not "earn out" the advance. *Book Number Two* not only earned out the advance, but also earned you an additional $5,000 in royalties. Here's the punchline: If your contracts allow cross-collateralization, your publisher will be able to keep the $5,000 *Book Number Two* earned and apply it to the unearned advance on *Book Number One*. A typical cross-collateralization clause states that earnings from a book can be applied to liabilities (the unearned advance) stemming from this "or any other" agreement. Translated, this means that all your royalties go into one big pot and the publisher can apply anything your books earn to any of your unearned balances.

Ironically, the beauty of an advance is that it is supposed to be nonrefund-

> **" If it can't hurt, it's gotta help."**
> **—Joe Parcella**

able. That's why it is always in the writer's best interest to get as big an advance as possible. But the cross-collateralization clause is a way for the publisher to get around the nonrefundable nature of the advance and not have to pay you what you've earned if one of your other books did not do very well.

A friend of mine learned about this clause the hard way: He lost thousands of dollars in royalties because his publisher applied earnings from a very successful book to one of his books that had been returned in droves. Read your contract. And cross out "or any other" and specifically ask the publisher to agree to its deletion. Personally, I consider cross-collateralization a deal-breaker. If you plan on writing more than one book for the same publisher, it is imperative that you make sure you're not burned later on by the application of this provision. If you can help it, **do not sign a contract with cross-collateralization.**

27. Reading postings on Internet newsgroups, surfing music Web sites, watching people on Webcams taking showers, or playing Snood online, is not research and it is not writing.

28. Subscribe to cable TV.

29. To minimize interruptions, decide when to pick up the phone by using caller ID as often as possible.

30. Wear loose-fitting clothing when you are writing.

31. "Write every day" is, of course, the ultimate writer's mantra. But you should be sure to also read something every day that is outside of your field of study and has nothing to do with what you're interested in at the moment. Read everything. Read the label of an iced tea bottle, the letter from the company president on the back of the potato chip bag, a comic

book, the section of *USA Today* you usually throw away, the copyright page of a book picked off the shelf at random, the grocery store flyer, the acknowledgments on your Dixie Chicks CD, the book club ads in *TV Guide*, the CD club ads in *Rolling Stone*, a page of a book of quotations, the warning on a bottle of Maalox tablets, a page from the Bible, the dirty jokes that were e-mailed to you a month ago, a page from your journal of two years ago, a recipe—the list could go on forever. Writers write, yes. But writers must also *read.* Regularly and voraciously.

32.   You can never have too many pads or mechanical pencils or highlighters.

33.   You may be the most brilliant writer since Charles Dickens, but you will still be edited—by at least one editor and possibly by several. This process may involve cutting material, being asked to rewrite stuff you thought was the perfect first time out, or even having your project completely rejected.

    I have a writer friend who has been writing professionally for decades and he just learned that his latest book was rejected by his editors. They requested a complete rewrite. (He may or may not oblige.) This also happened to Dava Sobel, the writer who wrote the enormously popular, best-selling nonfiction book *Longitude.* Her next book, however, *Galileo's Daughter*, was rejected in its first draft. Her editor asked for a complete rewrite according to his specifications and Sobel did as she was asked. She now admits that the revision made the book better. (And she once again had a huge best-seller.) You are not above being edited. Get used to it.

34.   You will never have enough storage space or bookshelf space. And someday you may actually move just to acquire more space for your books and files.

chapter 22

A Writer's FAQ:

16 Frequently Asked Questions About Writing Books and the Publishing Industry

Q I know I want to write, but I don't know where to begin.

A First, you need to determine what you want to write. Do you want to write a nonfiction book? Do you want to write short stories? A novel? Do you want to freelance for magazines? Do you want to give speeches about a beloved topic? Each of these areas of interest requires a different marketing strategy. Figure out what you want to say and then the right form of expression will come to you.

Q I've written a nonfiction book about the Korean War. I've also written a novel set in Korea. Should I just send my manuscripts to a publisher?

A Sure, if you like to waste postage and paper. Publishers rarely, if ever, are thrilled to see unsolicited submissions of complete manuscripts. Many of the big publishing houses return unsolicited manuscripts unopened. Some even have a rubber stamp for the envelope that

reads "Returned Unopened and Unread" (in red) to protect them from charges of thievery down the road. No, the best way to sell a book to a publisher these days is through the query letter approach.

What, pray tell, is the query letter approach?

You write an acquisitions editor a one- to four-page letter describing your book and asking if he or she would like to see more. Your query letter should describe the book in detail. Explain why you have the credentials to write it (or the amount of in-depth research you have done to write the book), who the audience for the book is, and what (if any) is the book's competition (very important). You conclude by offering the editor one of two things: a look at the complete manuscript or a "publisher's package." This consists of a detailed outline/table of contents for the book and the first 50 or so pages of the manuscript (this compilation of materials is collectively called the proposal). This approach—proposing to write the book—is the wisest strategy, even if the book is already written. More and more books are being sold by proposal these days and editors do not have time to read more than a few pages about a project. Besides, most editors can decide immediately if your project is something they would like to see more of or if it is not something their house would be interested in publishing. You can see how this approach saves everybody involved time and money and allows you to get your pitch out to several publishers at once. In addition, this works equally well for both fiction and nonfiction.

How do I know which editors to send my query letters to?

 There is an invaluable resource, found in every library in America, titled *Writer's Market*. It is published annually and it lists thousands of publishers in the United States and organizes these companies by category. Why is *Writer's Market*

published? To prevent you from sending a cookbook to a publisher that only publishes military histories. (This is done every day by writers who do not take the time to research the industry.) Books are merchandise and, as we discussed earlier, books are placed in categories in bookstores. It is not a quirky coincidence that certain publishers specialize in certain types of books and that books are placed in specific departments in the bookstore. This is how the industry works. If you have paid attention to my system, then you have defined your book by its category: military history, religion, cookbook, film, science, European history, sports, business, whatever. Once you know this, you can then go through *Writer's Market* and make a list of all the publishers that publish your type of book. Then, you must read through the detailed company profiles provided in *Writer's Market* and decide which companies are best suited to your type of book, and also how they want to be approached. Most publishers will ask to query first. Abide by this. Some will ask you to send the complete manuscript (although this is becoming rarer and rarer). Even in these instances, I recommend querying the editor first. It's easier, quicker, and just because a publisher is willing to accept a complete manuscript does not mean he or she will. It just means more photocopying, postage, and ultimately a shopworn-looking manuscript. Querying first is the more efficient way to go.

What are my chances of getting published?

In the past few years, the odds have been running 60 to 1 against your chances of getting a book published.

How can you quantify it so specifically? After all, my book is special and surely the odds against what *I've* written can not be that high!

Here's how those odds are calculated. The 12,000 or so publishers in the United States receive approximately 3,000,000 submissions a year. These 12,000 publishers buy and publish approximately 50,000 books a year. If you divide the submissions to publishers (3,000,000) by the published books (50,000) you come up with a rejection rate that averages out to 60 to 1 against. But there is a bright side.

Q: Three million submissions?! I'm depressed.

Listen: Every writer who dreams of being published has to keep one extremely important rule at the forefront of his or her mind at all times: Never take no for an answer. Persistence and determination are almost as important as industry and commitment. And all four are more important than talent. There are loads of talented people on this planet. It's those who refuse to accept defeat who end up being recognized.

Q: What's the aforementioned bright side?

Editors and publishers are *always* looking for the next great book, be it a novel or a nonfiction book. (Children's books exist in their own rarefied, highly specialized universe and the odds against an unknown writer selling a children's book are enormously higher than selling an adult-oriented book.) Even though 60 books are rejected for every one that's published, yours could be one of those that rises above the fray and is good and timely enough to secure a contract.

Q: Let's say I get a deal. How do I know when I've done enough research to write my book?

As I've discussed earlier, if you are digging deep and tracking down the articles, books, Web sites, and people necessary to adequately learn enough about your subject to write about it, you will invariably end up with more research material than you can possibly use. So to know when to stop hoarding data, I always schedule my workload and my application of the Six Steps based on my due date. For example, let's say you score a book deal and sign a contract that gives you nine months (approximately 200 work days) to research and write a 150,000 word book. When you actually sit down and start to write, you know that you are good for around 1,500 words a day of final text (factoring in simultaneous rewriting and editing). This means you will need a minimum of 100 work days to do the actual writing of your book. This leaves you with approximately 100 work days to do your research, review your materials, and take notes. Thus, after four or five months of accumulating materials and assimilating as much of the information as you can, the time will come to stop researching and start writing. These are only general guidelines, of course, but I think it is extremely helpful to actually schedule your writing, research, editing, and print-out times. Once you have a specific timetable, you can then adjust your days as necessary. But a good place to start is by writing out a day-by-day game plan.

What do you think of book signings?

Sometimes they're more trouble than they're worth. Book signings can be an ego booster, but only if people stop at your table, buy a book, and ask you to inscribe it to them. Many times an author will sit behind a stack of his or her books for the entire time of the signing and not sell or sign one book. I have had both experiences. I have done signings where the store sold dozens of my book, and the line for an autograph stretched the length of the store. I have also done signings where the store did not sell one book, and I sat there the entire time feeling embarrassed and humiliated. (These are not the aforementioned "ego-boosting" kind of book-signings.) If you are a big-name author and the publisher sends you on a book tour, then usually there will be advertisements and promotion in-store to assure a turn out. Sometimes, a publisher will send an unknown or little-known author on a book tour in the hopes of boosting sales by getting some publicity in the cities where he or she appears. This sounds like a good idea, but sometimes the author is simply given an itinerary and left to fend for him- or herself in the town where the signing takes place. Many authors have book tour horror stories, so pick and choose carefully where (and if) you choose to sign. The reality is that very often, a bookstore sponsors a book signing and no one shows. If you can handle that, then agree away! If this would bother your ego, then avoid book signings like the plague. Sorry to come across as so cynical, but I've walked through the fire on this one and know of what I speak...and many writer friends of mine have had similar experiences.

What should I know about Fair Use and copyrights?

Fair Use is the law that allows a writer to quote verbatim from another writer's work, within specific limits, in order to further the artistic merit of his or her own work. For instance, on page 51, I quote a paragraph from a novel by Stephen King in its entirety. The paragraph is relevant to the topic I am discussing and perfectly illustrates my point about the importance of defining and vividly describing locales in your writing.

Did you request permission from King to include this passage?

No.

Why not?

Because the passage is 155 words long and the accepted definition of Fair Use allows direct quoting up to 250 words, as long as the passage cited is less than 2 percent of the total word count of the source work. For example, if I quoted 155 words of a 500-word essay, I would be in violation, even though it was less than 250 words, because 155 words of a 500-word essay is 31 percent of the total piece and clearly exceeds the Fair Use law.

Should I copyright my book before I start offering it to publishers?

Absolutely not. It is nothing but a waste of time and money. You own the copyright on your work the moment it is created, regardless of whether or not you actually send a copy of the work along with the proper forms to the U. S. Copyright Office. You need not worry about being unprotected. If you sell your book, every publisher has a department (or at least a person) who handles acquiring copyrights for all the works the company publishes. Relax. If you get a deal, the publisher will take care of all that stuff for you. Worry instead about fine-tuning your book so that it is something a publisher would want to publish.

Do I need an agent?

Acquiring a literary agent these days is actually more difficult than being accepted by a publisher. Agents represent authors on spec. Therefore, the professional literary agents are exceptionally picky...and extremely busy. Concentrate on selling your book through the query letter approach. It will be far easier to get an agent to negotiate your contract and represent you once you have a serious offer from a publisher.

How can I make my book hit the best-seller list?

Tell you what: You figure that one out and let me know. In the meantime, just keep writing. If you do what you love, the money will follow. So do what you love. After all, that's why you write in the first place, isn't it?

chapter

23

An Interview with Acquisitions Editor Michael Lewis

First, let me put all my cards on the table and bow humbly to the gods of full disclosure: Mike Lewis has helped me get this book published. Mike has also been my editor for nine of my earlier books. Mike Lewis is also a friend and trusted adviser, as well as being a writer of talent and heart himself.

As I have discussed elsewhere in this volume, there have been moments when I was floundering while working on a book, unable to decide on a particular approach to the material; unable to decide whether or not to include a certain anecdote or chapter; or, horribly, doubting my original vision of a book. At that point I would always turn to Mike, spew my troubles on him, and await his always helpful answer. Sometimes, this would come in the form of a question. However, it was always the perfect question, and it inevitably set me back on track and got my stalled car back up and running again.

Mike is smart and savvy and possesses as demented a sense of humor as I do. That's why we get along so well, and why we've been friends for so many years, as well as being cre- ative partners in this bizarre endeavor known as book publishing. Although

174

if the day comes when Mike stops giving me book contracts, I'll drop him like a hot potato and put the malocchio on him for the next three millennia.

(Only kidding, Mike…or not.)

Mike's books as an author include *The Films of Harrison Ford, The Cheapskate's Guide to Walt Disney World, True Grits,* and *The Films of Tom Hanks.* He has also been in the publishing field for more than 10 years.

In the following interview, I ask Mike the questions I know he gets asked by beginning writers all the time. His answers are insightful, honest, and comprise a valuable insider's look at the book publishing industry.

•••

Steve Spignesi: What does an acquisitions editor do? Could you give us a description of a typical day in the life of an acquisitions editor for a publishing company?

Mike Lewis: What I like about my job is that each day has different experiences than the one before. On any given day, I could be: reading a manuscript, talking with authors I've worked with before about new ideas, negotiating contract terms with an agent or an author, generating my own ideas and researching where I might find the right author, brainstorming with sales and marketing staff about how to increase sales, opening unsolicited book proposals and evaluating them with the sales director and other acquisitions board members, working with potential authors on how to bolster their proposal in order to increase their chances of getting a book deal, reading trade publications and researching competition, following up with authors to make sure they're on track for their contracted delivery date, or calling agents to reject proposals they sent but perhaps offer them other ideas for which I'm seeking an author. Not all of these tasks are my favorite things to do, but their diversity ensures that I won't have to do something I dislike for too long. Being an acquisitions editor is definitely a good job for self-starters.

SS: How many submissions do you personally review in a month? How many do you pursue? Can you accept a book on your own if you really like the proposal?

ML: It's hard to estimate the number of submissions I get—probably 25 to 50 (or more) a month. I'll admit that I'm really too busy to personally review every submission. I will review every one, though, and I rarely reject it just based on my own initial feel for it (unless of course it's fiction, a cookbook, a humor book, among others—things I *know* we will not publish here). After I glance at it, I add it to the stack to prescreen with the associate publisher/ sales director. Ones that make it through that prescreen then go on the agenda at a future acquisitions meeting (usually held biweekly). People attending that meeting are myself, the sales director, special sales/rights director, the publisher, marketing director, publicity manager, and managing editor. They have all hopefully seen all of the proposals. Then we discuss their merit at the meeting. I have not been with this particular company (Career Press) long enough to know immediately if we should publish a book or not, but there are some that I feel strong about and will go to bat for. I'd estimate that approximately 93 percent of the books submitted will get rejected. Then I sit with the publisher and discuss contract terms for accepted books.

SS: What annoys you the most about writers who try to sell you a book?

ML: Phone calls can be annoying, or at least too many of them can get annoying. I cannot spend the time talking personally to everyone who's got a book idea, no matter what it might be. Even if I had all the time in the day to speak with every person, it would be impossible to say, "That sounds like a great idea! Don't even bother sending me the proposal! What's your address—I'll send a contract and your advance right out today!" I'm exaggerating, but I need to see that you can put together a winning proposal, because that will give me a little insight into your abilities to write a book.

SS: What is your personal preferred form of submission?

ML: I prefer having proposals or query letters mailed to me. If the potential author wants to spend the money to overnight it, hoping that by doing so it's going to get my utmost attention above all others, that's up to them. No book I've yet seen is that explosive that it can't wait a few days for the regular snail mail to bring it (but a potential author should always keep a copy in case it gets lost in mail limbo). Let me rank submission forms in order of my preference:

1. Mail.
2. E-Mail.
3. Fax.

Please don't use the phone (see above). And even if you're local, please don't stop by and drop off your proposal and expect me to have time to chat with you about it! (I don't want to come across as some grand and exalted ruler, but there aren't enough hours in the day to chat. That's why publishing is great for us introverts!)

SS: Have you ever completely rejected a book, resulting in it never being published by the company for which you were working at the time? Or do you always try and reshape the book so that it's publishable?

ML: I assume you mean a completed manuscript, not a proposal. I've never rejected a completed manuscript (although my publishers have, often for reasons of their own). And I don't expect I ever will reject a project I've signed. I'm pretty confident in the abilities of the people I contract with, and I am in contact with them once or twice between the time their contract is signed and the time their manuscript is due. I've already given them a contract based on their strong proposal, which showed me they could write pretty well. Sometimes, especially for first-time authors, I may build into their contract that part of their advance will be paid upon submission of a part of their manuscript—that way I can get a look at what they're doing while they're doing it, and refocus them if necessary before it's too late.

SS: Describe the perfect working relationship between you and a writer.

ML: My relationship with you, of course. (Spignesi nods eagerly, the perfect mid-list sycophant.) But seriously, my ideal relationship is one of a creative partnership. Never losing sight of who signs my paycheck, I view my relationship with an author as a partnership, soldiers going off to battle together. We can bounce ideas off each other and we are both thick-skinned enough to take some blunt criticism. We both have a common goal: to produce something to be proud of that will find its niche and sell.

SS: How do you handle the writer who refuses to make changes you suggest? Do you defer to the writer or does the writer have to accommodate your requests if he or she wants the book published?

ML: I'm reasonable—I am here to make suggestions that will make a book better, but I also realize the author's voice has to remain. Hopefully, the author is reasonable, too, and knows I have the same goal as they do—to make the book better—and that they'll defer to my judgment. I often have to explain my reasons for suggesting a change, and 99.9 percent of the time, I convince them, or we at least meet somewhere in the middle. And that other 0.1 percent of the time, I see their side and I let it go. Again, it all starts with signing decent, intelligent people to write for you, and building a rapport with them. It's not supposed to be adversarial, because that hinders creativity and excellence.

SS: What is a typical advance for a first-timer's nonfiction book these days? I know it's hard to be specific when not talking about an individual book, but what is the range in the industry? What can a first-book author expect to be offered?

ML: First time authors are usually given the basic contract, with most terms favoring the publisher. Once he or she builds a track record, and better understands what they've signed, some items can be ratcheted up in their favor. I really can't discuss average advances because I'm unaware what's going on outside my little world (being an introvert). But I've personally seen advances ranging from $500 to $500,000 and more. And some publishers don't pay advances at all, so even $500 from me might seem a lot to some authors. The reality first-timers face is that writing is a labor of love—if you divide the advance you're getting by the amount of hours it's taking you to write the book, you're earning pennies on the dollar. But if your book goes into reprint and gets backlisted, you can earn a living as a writer.

SS: Do you prefer dealing with a writer or an agent when it comes to contract terms?

ML: I realize the realities of today, and know the value of agents, especially for busy writers with multiple books and multiple deals with multiple publishers. But it's easier to work with less people. Most agents are nice, decent people, but I've encountered some that have an adversarial attitude. But an agent can be helpful in getting an author a better deal.

SS: What was the most successful book you ever edited?

ML: Only one book I have edited has hit the bestseller list, specifically your book, *JFK Jr.*, which hit number 16 on the extended *New York Times* bestseller list in the fall of 1999. I have also edited many that have become perennial backlist books. Many of these are in New Age genre, which is a very popular category these days.

SS: What was the least successful book you ever edited?

ML: It's hard to pinpoint which one. Thousands of new books are published every year. And as you might expect, the majority of them tank. And I've had my share of well-intentioned failures. And you often never know why.

SS: To conclude, if you could offer an unpublished writer only one piece of advice, what would it be?

ML: I would probably say to keep working. Keep a pad and paper with you at all times, and when something pops into your head (a book idea, an idea for an addition to something you've already written) jot it down. Stay organized. Don't get discouraged if you get some rejections—keep at it. There are so many publishers, you're bound to find the perfect match. And once you get a deal, start writing from the moment you get your contract—don't wait until the last minute. That due date looks so far off, but before you know it, it will be tomorrow and your editor is going to say, "I look forward to getting it." And you'll probably scream! (Sorry, that was more than one bit of advice. I couldn't help myself.)

c o d a

What It's Like to Be the Author of a Bestseller

(and not get any money for it)

❝ *I have a bone to pick with Fate...* **❞**

—Ogden Nash

J ohn F. Kennedy Jr., his wife Carolyn Bessette-Kennedy, and Carolyn's sister, Lauren Bessette, all died on July 16, 1999 when the plane John was piloting crashed into the Atlantic Ocean off Martha's Vineyard.

Ironically, that tragedy is the single event that has most impacted my writing career (so far) and the event that gave me my first *New York Times* bestseller. A *New York Times* best-seller is the gold standard for gauging a writer's success. It is also every writer's dream to have a *New York Times* bestseller.

In the fall of 1999, my book *JFK Jr.* hit number 16 on the extended *Times* best-seller list. (*The Times* only publishes the top 15 titles on the weekly best-seller list that appears in *The New York Times Book Review*. They actually rank many more titles than 15, though, and they publish the complete list on their Web site. My book hit number 16 on this extended list. I was only one ranking away from making the book review listing.)

Prior to that milestone, the book had jumped from around number 168,000 on *Amazon.com* to a peak of

181

number 4 on the Internet bookseller's best-selling books list. In addition, *JFK Jr.* had hit number 1 on the Ingram trade list.

The day John F. Kennedy's plane was reported missing—July 16, 1999—was a Saturday, and my 46th birthday. My book about John— then titled *The JFK Jr. Scrapbook*—had been out for almost two and a half years and had sold a piddling 9,500 copies during that entire period.

That tragic Saturday, by three in the afternoon the book had shot up to number 21 on Amazon. By that time I had already given my first interview about John, a live chat with an Australian radio station that had been able to track me down on a weekend when my publisher's office was closed and my unpublished phone number was nowhere to be found.

That was only the beginning of a whirlwind month that would include live interviews at all hours of the day and night on CNN, MSNBC, Fox News, and other TV and radio outlets, both in the U.S. and around the world. There followed the print interviews with the *Chicago Tribune*, Associated Press, the *Boston Globe, The New York Times, The New Haven Register*, and too many others to remember.

The few remaining copies of the first edition of my book (the one titled *The JFK Jr. Scrapbook*) sold out the day John was reported missing, and I immediately began accumulating press clippings, magazines, and other materials I knew I would need for a second edition.

We eventually went back to press for an 85,000 copy print run of the second edition, now simply titled *JFK Jr.* For that edition, I deleted a "JFK Jr. word search puzzle" and added a complete account of the accident, the search, the recovery, the burial at sea, and the memorial services. It was this edition that hit the *Times* best-seller list.

So how did it feel to have my first best-seller? How did it feel to have my ultimate writer's dream fulfilled?

To answer, allow me to cite an excerpt from an article by Jim Shelton in the *New Haven Register* about me that ran shortly before the book hit the *Times* best-seller list. The piece is titled "Best-Seller Blues."

> *This wasn't how Stephen Spignesi wanted to have a hit book.*
> *He's always been a pop culture guy, a nostalgia guy. He writes about fun topics, such as TV shows, UFOs, and horror novelist Stephen King.*

Yet here he is with a hit book coming out in a second edition, and it's the most awkward time in his professional career. It's his 1997 book on John Kennedy Jr., whose death last month shocked the nation and sent thousands of people to bookstores looking for Spignesi's book.

"It's beyond irony," the 46-year-old New Haven author says. "I'm of course pleased to have a book sell well, but who wants it this way? I'm not reveling in this. I won't."

Spignesi's book came out in January 1997 to less-than-stellar sales. "It didn't tank, but it didn't do well," he says. "I think people took for granted that he'd always be there."

Spignesi went on to other projects, including a 1998 book, Young Kennedys, under the pen name Jay David Andrews.

Then in July, Kennedy's plane crashed at sea near Martha's Vineyard, killing him, his wife and his sister-in-law.

Spignesi's book suddenly became hot. Radio stations, TV crews, newspapers and magazines all sought him out for comment. Friends called to tell him that people were offering copies of the book on the Internet for up to $200.

One disc jockey asked him on the air if he was glad Kennedy had died, so he could sell more books.

"Look, this book is two and a half years old," Spignesi says. "It was a passive success. I've never pitched an idea about someone who died."

Now, almost a year after Kennedy's death, my book is still in the stores, although sales have trickled off to almost nothing and the distributor has gotten some returns from stores that did not sell what they ordered.

It was an exhilarating experience having a best-seller and being sought after by the media and being on TV and in the papers.

But sometimes the universe works in mysterious ways: The publisher of *JFK Jr.* filed for bankruptcy shortly after getting paid for the sale of my books. This resulted in all monies earned by the company going into one big pool of assets that were eventually auctioned off. My net share of the proceeds? My *JFK Jr.*, royalties amounted to less than 10 cents on the dollar earned by the book.

So that's what it's like to write a best-selling book and not receive any money for it. The universe sometimes works in unusual ways, wouldn't you agree?

The Final Word: Stephen King on Writing

riting isn't about making money, getting famous, getting dates, getting laid, or making friends. In the end, it's about enriching the lives of those who will read your work, and enriching your own life, as well. It's about getting up, getting well, and getting over. Getting happy, okay? Getting happy....Writing is magic, as much the water of life as any other creative art. The water is free. So drink.

Drink and be filled up.

From *On Writing: A Memoir of the Craft* by Stephen King (Scribner, 2000)

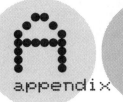

Looking for Lincolns
A Search for Information About Abraham Lincoln and His Sons

 When you're writing, you're trying to find out something which you don't know.

—James Baldwin

 ne of the first steps in assembling your research materials—regardless of the subject you are writing about—should be an Internet search. And as I've already discussed, access to the Internet is essential these days for authors, students, speakers, whomever, in order to facilitate the research process. A few years ago, this was not the case. The Internet was nowhere near as organized as it is today; nor did the World Wide Web offer the extensive range of materials, documents, information, and Web sites available today.

Let me illustrate this point: In 1999, I wrote a book called *The USA Book of Lists*. One of the features in the book was a list called "The 10 Greatest American Speeches of the 20th Century." A group of experts in rhetoric (under the auspices of the University of Wisconsin) had culled through hundreds of speeches given from 1900 through the year 2000. They determined the greatest speeches of the century based primarily on their influence and artistry. They published their complete list of the winners

and, for my book, I decided to write about, and run excerpts from, the top 10.

The top speech of the 10 was Martin Luther King's "I Have a Dream" speech. The rest of the top 10 included Ronald Reagan's Challenger eulogy, FDR's "Day of Infamy" and "Fear Itself" speeches, JFK's inaugural address ("Ask not..."), along with speeches written by Barbara Jordan, Lyndon Johnson, Richard Nixon, and Malcolm X. It was a very impressive array of brilliant speeches. I was familiar with most of them, and felt that this would make an interesting and informative feature for my book. The problem, however, was that I did not have the texts of even one of the speeches, and it had been years since I had either heard or read them.

But the power of the Internet came through for me.

Using only one search engine (Google) I was able to locate the complete texts of all 10 speeches and download them to my hard drive to read and study later.

My total time online for this expedition? A nice and speedy 32 minutes.

Prior to the easy accessibility of the Internet, I would have had to go to the library, find the texts of the speeches in books or sources (such as newspapers on microfilm or microfiche) and then either photocopy or print out the pages. To acquire all 10 speeches could easily have taken an entire day at a good public or university library. (That is if your library of choice actually *had* all 10 speeches.) The valuable materials you are seeking all exist out there, hidden away in libraries and archives all over the country, but finding them and then using them is where the problems arise...and where scads of time is wasted.

In many cases, the Internet can be a godsend and an incredible timesaver. Searching the Internet, however, can also be time-consuming, frustrating, confusing, boring, surreal, and tremendously distracting. It's very tempting to click on a Web site that sounds interesting, even if it was returned to you in error during a search and has nothing to do with what you're looking for.

I will now look at these contrasting aspects of the Internet and explore ways to cut through the nonsense and get right to the materials you need for your work. Together, we will work our way through an Internet search for materials (related to the sons of Abraham Lincoln, of course). Later, we will do a comprehensive review of the *Reader's Guide to Periodical Literature.*

The Internet

To get started in acquiring general Abraham Lincoln info, I started by searching the World Wide Web using four powerful and popular search engines: **AltaVista**, **Excite**, **Google**, and **Infoseek**. I used the search engine resident on the *iWon.com* Internet sweepstakes site (which is produced by CBS). I also searched using the "subject tree" search engine, Magellan.

> *The Net has empowered us, given us the tools we need to find information and make decisions, large and small, about our lives. It's eliminated the middleman. It's done away with the need to wait in line, whether at the public library or in voice-mail limbo, until it's our turn to have our questions answered. The Net has given us instant research gratification—assuming, that is, that we can actually find what we're looking for online.*
>
> **—Reva Basch**

Following these searches, I then searched *bn.com* (Barnes & Noble's Web site) for a list of books-in-print about Abraham Lincoln. Then I went to *Bibliofind.com* for a list of out-of-print books about Lincoln. (It was on the Bibliofind site that I found a dealer who had the invaluable 1955 biography *Lincoln's Sons*, which I purchased for $4—I'll talk about this later.)

When I begin the research for a book, I usually search using many more search engines than the few excerpted here, but I think these will work for illustrative and sampling purposes.

In this section, I reproduce a listing of the first 10 results returned by each search engine. Then I comment on which results I would consider important for general information about Lincoln. This kind of evaluation process should be applied to your subject. Approach your search critically, with an eye towards advancing your base of knowledge regarding your subject. Search engine results are notoriously fickle—sometimes the *strangest* sites are found. You need to learn how to quickly reject the useless results.

After searching using the engines mentioned, I then refined my search, using one search engine (*Google.com*) to search for Lincoln's sons by name, and those annotated results follow the section on the general "Abraham Lincoln" results.

AltaVIsta (www.altavista.com)

Web Pages: 80,721 pages found.

1. IPL POTUS — Abraham Lincoln

The Internet Public Library. Links immediately following the image of the American Flag are links to other POTUS sites. All other links lead to...

URL: *www.ipl.org/ref/POTUS/allncoln.html*

2. Encyclopedia Americana: Abraham Lincoln

Inaugural Address I Quick Facts I The Presidents I EA Contents I ABRAHAM LINCOLN Biography. Abraham Lincoln (1809-1865), 16th PRESIDENT OF THE UNITED...

URL: *gi.grolier.com/presidents/ea/bios/16plinc.html*

3. Abraham Lincoln: Second Inaugural Address. U.S. Inaugural Addresses. 1989 Bartleby.com. —— Reference. Verse. Fiction. Nonfiction. —— Dictionary. Roget's II: Thesaurus. Simpson's Quotations. English Usage. Columbia...

URL: *www.bartleby.com/124/pres32.html*

4. Abraham Lincoln Online Search Engine

Use this form to search pages on Abraham Lincoln Online! Search Text: Home Pages... Writings (ALO) Mailbag—> (select one) Home I News I Sites I...

URL: *www.netins.net/showcase/creative/lincoln/search.htm*

5. The History Place - Abraham Lincoln

Proclamation Calling Militia and Convening Congress - Part of our Lincoln Timeline....

URL: *www.historyplace.com/lincoln/proc-1.htm*

6. Abraham Lincoln - 16th President of the United States

Lucidcafe's profile of Abraham Lincoln...

URL: *www2.lucidcafe.com/lucidcafe/library/96feb/lincoln.html*

7. Abraham Lincoln Camps * Living history at it's best

Ralph E. Borror is a living historian has been presenting as Abraham Lincoln the 16th President for over 11 years...

URL: *www.abraham-lincoln.net*

8. Abraham Lincoln - 16th President of the United States

Lucidcafe's profile of Abraham Lincoln...

URL: *www.lucidcafe.com/library/96feb/lincoln.html*

9. On Abraham Lincoln

Library: Historical Documents: Robert Ingersoll: On Abraham Lincoln. Order books by and about Robert Ingersoll now. On Abraham Lincoln. Robert Green...

URL: *www.infidels.org/library/historical/robe.*

10. Abraham Lincoln Brigade Archives - Home Page

Mark your calendar! - Baltazar Garzon will deliver the Third ALBA-Bill Susman lecture at NYU, April 28, 2000 — "Millennial Tribute to Our Vets,"...

URL: *www.alba-valb.org*

•••

Have you tried these resources?

- Comparison shop for Abraham-Lincoln.
- Get expert advice on Abraham-Lincoln at EXP.
- Shop by request for Abraham-Lincoln at *Respond.com.*
- For Yellow Page information visit WorldPages.
- Search no more! Get to know Abraham-Lincoln at *Britannica.com.*
- Narrow your search on Abraham-Lincoln with LookSmart Categories.

Because we're doing a range of projects about Lincoln's sons, my initial reaction to AltaVista's top 10 Lincoln sites is that there isn't much here to use. **The Internet Public Library** would probably be a good jumping-off point for other Lincoln sites and **The Abraham Lincoln Online** search engine is worth checking out as well (I would search for Lincoln's sons by name). The other sites do not look promising for the kind of information we're looking for. Interestingly, you would think that AltaVista's "Have you tried these resources?" appendix would expand access to sources, but in this case it is essentially useless for our purposes.

Excite (www.excite.com)

Select words to add to your search:

lincolns   southerners

surratt   exonerate

assassination   diesen

daguerreotype   abe

assassinated   proclamation

Education > Arts & Humanities > History > Military History & Wars > 19th Century > Civil War

Top 10 matches.

76% Abraham Lincoln Brigade Archives

www.alba-valb.org/

73% The Abraham Lincoln Association

Welcome to the Abraham Lincoln Association - The Abraham Lincoln Association was organized in 1908 as the Lincoln Centennial Association. It led the national celebration of Lincoln's one-hundredth birthday and continued to mark that day until 1925, when Paul M....

www.alincolnassoc.com/

73% Abraham Lincoln

This pictorial history of Abraham Lincoln has been published by students of... Berwick Academy Class of 2008 © Berwick Academy First Grade, South Berwick, Maine: March, 1997

www.berwickacademy.org/lincoln/lincoln.htm

72% Abraham Lincoln: A Leader of Honor

Abraham Lincoln: A Leader of Honor "I am decided; my course is fixed; my path is blazed. The Union and the Constitution shall be preserved and the laws enforced at every and at all hazards."

www.abrahamlincoln.cc/

72% The Lincoln Museum

General Grant B. General Sherman C. General Motors D. General McClellan Copyright © 1996 The Lincoln Museum Please visit the Museum Index at...

www.thelincolnmuseum.org/museum_index.html

www.thelincolnmuseum.org/main.html

71% Abraham Lincoln Camps * Living history at it's best

Ralph E. Borror is a living historian has been presenting as Abraham Lincoln the 16th President for over 10 years...

www.abraham-lincoln.net/

70% Lincoln Portrait - Early Daguerreotype of Abraham Lincoln

Daguerreotype portrait of young Abraham Lincoln, likely made in Louisville, KY in 1841, one of the earliest photographic images. Framed photographic prints are available.

www.lincolnportrait.com/

70% Top Seven Abraham Lincoln Books

This list exists to help the new Lincoln and/or Civil War enthusiast put together a great compact Lincoln library. Why seven? Books about Abraham Lincoln have been cranked out like sausages since 1865, some good, some great, some poor.

www.liqua.com/lincoln/

70% Red Rock Elementary - Abraham Lincoln

Abraham Lincoln - The History Place presents Abraham Lincoln - Civil War - House Divided Speech - Information on Abraham Lincoln - Abraham Lincoln Online - Lincoln Legal Papers

www.rr.gmcs.k12.nm.us/domagala.alincoln.htm

70% NEW HERALD - LINCOLN HERALD edited by THOMAS R.

Welcome to the LINCOLN HERALD a publication of Lincoln Memorial University located in Harrogate, Tennessee. The Herald is published four times a year and is devoted to publishing articles related to the life and times of Abraham Lincoln.

Web.mountain.net/~niddk/index.htm

•••

First, none of the "select words to add to your search" suggested by Excite would help us in our research about Lincoln's family. As for the top 10 Web sites that Excite found, the only one that would probably be useful for our purposes is the **"Top Seven Abraham Lincoln Books"** site. These titles will more than likely contain information about Lincoln's children and his family life. I would visit this site, note the titles, and then pursue each one further to determine whether or not they were helpful. Also, the ***Lincoln Herald*** site would be worth glancing at because sometimes these kinds of publications have interesting, offbeat articles about their subjects.

Google (www.google.com)

1-10 of about 43,100 for Abraham-Lincoln

Search took 0.22 seconds.

Category: Society > History > United States > Presidents > Lincoln, Abraham

1. Abraham Lincoln Online

... Abraham Lincoln Online Lincoln This Week Speeches/Writings...

Description: Extensive collection of Lincoln resources, including on-line versions of his speeches...

Category: Society > History > United States > Presidents > Lincoln, Abraham www.netins.net/showcase/creative/lincoln.html

2. Abraham Lincoln Research Site

...teacher who enjoys researching Abraham Lincoln's life and...

Description: Aimed at families and students studying Abraham Lincoln's life, his family, his accomplish...

Category: Society > History > United States > Presidents > Lincoln, Abraham

members.aol.com/RVSNorton/Lincoln2.html

3. Abraham Lincoln Assassination

...particularly interested in Abraham Lincoln's assassination.

Description: Complete coverage of the assassination of Abraham Lincoln is provided by this Web site...

Category: Society > History > Presidents > Lincoln, Abraham > Assassination

members.aol.com/RVSNorton/Lincoln.html

4. IPL POTUS — Abraham Lincoln

...Resources I Points of Interest Abraham Lincoln 16th President of...

Description: Presidential facts, from election results to points of interest, at the Internet Public...

Category: Society > History > United States > Presidents > Lincoln, Abraham

www.ipl.org/ref/POTUS/alincoln.html

5. Abraham Lincoln

...Abraham Lincoln Sixteenth President 1861-1865 [Mary Todd...

Description: Brief biography, speeches and quotes from the White House's official site.

Category: Society > History > United States > Presidents > Lincoln, Abraham

www.whitehouse.gov/WH/glimpse/presidents/html/al16.html

6. The History Place presents Abraham Lincoln

...Massachusetts. 1778 - Thomas Lincoln (Abraham's father),...

...Kentucky. Feb. 12, 1809 - Abraham Lincoln is born in a one room...

www.historyplace.com/lincoln/ - Cached - 32k - GoogleScout

7. The Abraham Lincoln Association

...Welcome to the Abraham Lincoln Association

Description: Hosts a fully-searchable online version of Lincoln's collected works.

Category: Society > History > United States > Presidents > Lincoln, Abraham

www.alincolnassoc.com/

8. Abraham Lincoln for Primary Children

...first grade class visits Abraham Lincoln's Boyhood National...

...facts they've learned about Abraham Lincoln. take an on-line quiz...

www.siec.k12.in.us/~west/proj/lincoln/

194 / Instant Expert

9. Abraham Lincoln Birthplace National Historic Site Home Page
... Abraham Lincoln Birthplace National Historic Site In the fall of...
Description: Official NHS site
Category: Regional > North America > Abraham Lincoln Birthplace NHS
www.nps.gov/abli/
10. Encyclopedia Americana: Abraham Lincoln
...Presidents I EA Contents I ABRAHAM LINCOLN Biography...
...In an autobiography that Abraham Lincoln composed in 1860, he said...
gi.grolier.com/presidents/ea/bios/16plinc.html

•••

Google is usually an excellent search engine for quick and accurate results. The 10 "Lincoln" results cited here prove this quite dramatically. I would immediately visit the **"Abraham Lincoln Online"** site, the **"Abraham Lincoln Research Site,"** the **"Abraham Lincoln"** site, **"The History Place presents Abraham Lincoln"** site, and the **"Abraham Lincoln Birthplace National Historic Site Home Page."** Of course this does not mean that these sites would serve to advance our research goals; you can only determine that by reviewing them. However, they do seem to be quite targeted for our needs: biographical information about Abraham Lincoln with a focus on his sons and family life. We will revisit Google later for "son-specific" searching, but for now these sites are a good jumping-off place for basic research.

Infoseek (www.infoseek.com)

www.infoseek.com
20,030 matches
1. Abraham Lincoln Online
Everything about Honest Abe, from speeches to photographs and a Quiz of the Month. You can even join an online discussion.
Relevance: 94%
www.netins.net/showcase/creative/lincoln.html
2. Abraham Lincoln Research Site
Basic site about Abraham Lincoln, with a biography, poems, and facts about the assassination.
Relevance: 94%

members.aol.com/RVSNorton/Lincoln2.html

3. POTUS: Abraham Lincoln

Site with background information, election results, cabinet members, notable events, and some points of interest on Abraham Lincoln.

Relevance: 93%

www.ipl.org/ref/POTUS/alincoln.html

4. The History Place presents Abraham Lincoln

Includes a detailed Timeline of Lincoln's life - Photos of Lincoln and all the major personalities from the Civil War - Info on the Battle of Gettysburg, Kansas-Nebraska Act, Dred Scott ...

Relevance: 91%

www.historyplace.com/lincoln/index.html

5. Lincoln 1863 Thanksgiving Proclamation

From the collection of Lincoln's papers in the Library of America series, Vol II, pp. 520-521. The year that is drawing towards its close, has been filled with the blessings of fruitful ...

Relevance: 90%

tristate.pgh.net/~garyr/linc_doc.html

6. Abraham Lincoln

Official information site on Abraham Lincoln from the White House.

Relevance: 89%

www.whitehouse.gov/WH/glimpse/presidents/html/al16.html

7. Abraham Lincoln Birthplace NHS Home Page

Abraham Lincoln Birthplace National Historic Site

In the fall of 1808, Thomas and Nancy Lincoln settled on the 348 acre Sinking Spring Farm. Two months later on February 12, 1809, Abraham Lincoln was born ...

Relevance: 89%

www.nps.gov/htdocs2/abli/index.htm

8. U.S. Navy - The Aircraft Carrier

Since World War II, the U.S. Navy's carriers have been the national force of choice. Information, images and a brief history of the aircraft carrier.

Relevance: 87%

www.chinfo.navy.mil/navpalib/ships/carriers/

9. Lincoln High School (San Jose)

General school information.

Relevance: 87%

143.254.50.40/

10. Abraham Lincoln for Primary Children

Here's a Web-based activity about Abraham Lincoln for primary age children.
Relevance: 84%

www.siec.k12.in.us/~west/proj/lincoln/index.html

•••

We're now beginning to see some duplication—some of the same sites are being returned. I would probably revisit the ones I listed in my Google results. There really isn't much else here in Infoseek's top 10, although I may have clicked through to a few more pages of results just to see what else they have found. After all, the search engine did come back with over 20,000 results, but usually the most visited and/or most relevant are the top 10 to 20 listed.

iWon (www.iWon.com)

50,809 results

1. Abraham Lincoln Online

Abraham Lincoln Online - Abraham Lincoln Online - Lincoln This Week - Speeches/Writings - Historic Places - Lincoln Resources Book - Discussion - News and Events - Lincoln Mailbag - Educational Links - Lincoln Bookshelf - Search ALO Frequently Asked Lincoln Questions

Location: www.netins.net/showcase/creative/lincoln.html

2. Abraham Lincoln for Primary Children

Abraham Lincoln for Primary Children Animated Gifs by The Wagontrain Copyright © 1996 All Rights Reserved.

every year our first grade class visits Abraham Lincoln's Boyhood National Memorial at Lincoln City, Indiana. This activity is...

Location: www.siec.k12.in.us/~west/proj/lincoln

3. The History Place presents Abraham Lincoln

The History Place presents Abraham Lincoln - Jump To: Lincoln becomes President - Emancipation Proclamation - Battle of Gettysburg - Kansas-Nebraska Act - Dred Scott Decision 1637 - Samuel Lincoln from Hingham, England settles in Hingham, Mass...

Location: www.historyplace.com/lincoln

4. Abraham Lincoln Research Site

Abraham Lincoln Research Site

I am not an author or an historian; rather I am a former American history teacher who enjoys researching Abraham Lincoln's life and accomplishments. If you have a specific Lincoln question that you would...

Location: members.aol.com/RVSNorton/Lincoln2.html

5. Abraham Lincoln

Abraham Lincoln - Abraham Lincoln - Abraham Lincoln - Abraham Lincoln Online - This page has links to LOTS of great Lincoln information, including: Historic sites, speeches and writings, pictures, a quiz, Lincoln Birthday events and more! A biography of...

Location: deil.lang.uiuc.edu/Web.pages/holidays/Lincoln.html

6. Abraham Lincoln

Abraham Lincoln - Abraham Lincoln Sixteenth President 1861-1865 [Mary Todd Lincoln]

Fun Fact: During the Civil War, telegraph wires were strung to follow the action on the battlefield. But there was no telegraph office in the White House, so Lincoln...

Location: www.whitehouse.gov/WH/glimpse/presidents/html/al16.html

7. Abraham Lincoln Brigade Archives - Home Page

Abraham Lincoln Brigade Archives - Home Page - About ALBA - Dialog - Exhibits - Bookstore - Education - Links - The Volunteer - VALB - ALBA Archives - Screen Saver - Events

Location: www.alba-valb.org/

8. Abraham Lincoln

This pictorial history of Abraham Lincoln has been published by students of Berwick Academy Class of 2008 © Berwick Academy First Grade, South Berwick, Maine: March, 1997. The Illustrated Timeline - Read a biography of Abraham Lincoln

Location: www.berwickacademy.org/lincoln/lincoln.htm

9. Abraham Lincoln: An Educational Site

Welcome to all of Mr. Donovan's students and other visitors. There is a lot of information available on this site about Abraham Lincoln, our nation's 16th President. I hope that you enjoy this site.

Location: www.geocities.com/SunsetStrip/Venue/5217/lincoln.html

10. IPL POTUS — Abraham Lincoln

IPL POTUS — Abraham Lincoln the Internet Public Library - Links immediately following the image of the American Flag are links to other POTUS sites. All other links lead to sites elsewhere on the Web. Jump to: Presidential Election Results

Location: www.ipl.org/ref/POTUS/alincoln.html

MATCHING NEWS ARTICLES 1-3 (of 3)

Redherring.com - IPO month ahead: April not foolin' for $13.5 billion- April 03, 2000. The week of April 3 has 24 IPOs scheduled, with an expected dollar volume of $7.4 billion. The new-issues market expects to raise $13.5 billion from 80 offerings during the month of April.

Latest news from CNNfn - search cnnfn - the Web - stock quote - News - deals & debuts - technology companies - Markets - track your stocks - bonds & rates - morning call - ipos - Retirement - mutual funds - strategies - 401(k)s and IRAs - Consumer home & auto investing...

The Awful Truth About the Dime Museum - Print Edition - Style - Articles - Weekend Section - Front Page - Articles On Our Site Museums & Galleries - Theater & Dance - Visitors' Guide Style Live The Awful Truth About the Dime Museum By Michael O'Sullivan, Washington Post Staff Writer - Friday, April 7

•••

iWon came back with more than 50,000 results, but they are all more of the same sites returned by the other search engines. And the "Matching News Articles" feature returned with most searches is utterly irrelevant.

Magellan Internet Guide (www.magellan.com)

1. 76% Abraham Lincoln Brigade Archives - Home Page
www.alba-valb.org/
2. 72% Abraham Lincoln: A Leader of Honor
www.abrahamlincoln.cc/
3. 72% The Lincoln Museum
www.thelincolnmuseum.org/main.html
4. 71% Abraham Lincoln Camps * Living history at it's best
www.abraham-lincoln.net/
5. 70% Lincoln Portrait - Early Daguerreotype of Abraham Lincoln
www.lincolnportrait.com/
6. 70% Welcome To ALULAW.COM
www.alulaw.com/
7. 69% The Lincolnia Web Page
home.earthlink.net/~lincolnia/index.html
8. 69% The Rail Splitter
www.railsplitter.com/

A Journal for the Lincoln Collector and Market for Buying and Selling Historical Americana - Welcome to The Rail Splitter Home Page - The Rail Splitter is a national organization of collectors, dealers and scholars interested in Lincoln and the material culture of the period.

9. 69% Untitled

members.tripod.com/~greatamericanhistory/index.html

10. 69% City of Springfield, Illinois U.S.A.

www.springfield.il.us/

•••

Magellan is a "subject tree" type of search engine that is supposed to find related subjects and sites based on your search term. Northern Light, Yahoo!, AltaVista, and other search engines now do the same thing and I have found that in many cases they provide more cogent and useful results than Magellan. I find Northern Light especially helpful.

Oodles of Google

As you may have figured out by now, I really like Google a lot. (So do a lot of other people—Google won the 1999 Webby Award for best search engine.) I do not like to waste time on the Internet with search engines that have to load up dozens of category links and graphics and other nonsense before you are allowed to search. Combine all that flotsam with slow modems and a sluggish Internet and you can waste all kinds of time doing nothing but waiting. Google's site gives you a search box and two search buttons. And it's lightning-fast. In fact, its "I'm Feeling Lucky" button will automatically take you to the first site it finds, saving even more time. The big boys could take a lesson from the "new kid on the block," Google.

But back to our Lincoln search.

After compiling our list of Lincoln Web sites that provide general biographical information about the 16th president, we can now narrow our search for specific information about each of Lincoln's four sons. I started with the eldest of Abe's boy, Robert, and searched on Google for Robert-Todd-Lincoln. I put dashes between the names so that Google would only find me sites on which all three words were in sequence (this is known as a "search string"), thereby preventing it from returning a list of every Web site on which the name "Robert" is found; or "Todd," or "Lincoln." Here are the top ten sites Google returned for this search:

1-10 results of about 555 for

"Robert Todd Lincoln"

Search took 0.11 seconds.

1. Hildene - Historic Home of Robert Todd Lincoln in

... ROBERT TODD LINCOLN'S MANCHESTER, VERMONT You're always...

Description: Historic summer home of Robert Todd Lincoln in Manchester, Vermont.

www.hildene.org/

2. The Lincoln Family

... Robert Todd Lincoln's Hildene, Historic Rt. 7A...Manchester, Vermont Robert Todd Lincoln & the...

www.hildene.org/LincolnFamily.htm

3. Robert Lincoln

...Collection Photographs Robert Todd Lincoln, Abraham and...Beckwith (1898-1975) and Robert Todd Lincoln Beckwith...

home.att.net/~rjnorton/Lincoln66.html

4. Mary Todd Lincoln Biography

...for $4.00 a week. 1843 Robert Todd Lincoln, the couple's...Myra Bradwell. LEFT: Robert Todd Lincoln RIGHT: Bellevue...

members.aol.com/RVSNorton/Lincoln16.html

5. Encyclopedia Americana: Mary Todd Lincoln

...but only the oldest, Robert Todd Lincoln, lived to...take her own life, Robert Todd Lincoln brought insanity...

gi.grolier.com/presidents/ea/first/16pw.html

6. The Political Graveyard: Index to Politicians: Lewison to Lindquist

politicalgraveyard.com/bio/ley-lindq.html

7. Robert Todd Lincoln, Captain, United States Army

... Robert Todd Lincoln Captain, United States Army &...& Secretary of War Robert Todd Lincoln (August 1,...

www.arlingtoncemetery.com/robertto.htm

8. Grave of Robert Todd Lincoln

...Advertisement Robert Todd Lincoln Son of Abraham...

www.findagrave.com/pictures/628.html

9. Robert Todd Lincoln

... LINCOLN HOME NATIONAL HISTORIC SITE Robert Todd...named after Mary's father, Robert Smith Todd. As Robert...

www.nps.gov/liho/family/robert.htm

10. Robert Todd Lincoln Tomb

... Robert Todd Lincoln Tomb Arlington National Cemetery...can see the tomb of

Robert Todd Lincoln by taking a short...
www.netins.net/showcase/creative/lincoln/sites/robert.htm

•••

Now we're cooking with gas, eh? Just these 10 results alone will undoubtedly provide a plethora of valuable information about Lincoln's eldest son. Then, I then moved on to the Lincolns' second born, Eddie. The results:

1-10 results of about 76 for
"Eddie Lincoln"
Search took 0.70 seconds.
1. Eddie Lincoln
,..photograph of Eddie was first published in 1998 in Lincoln's...custodian of the Lincoln Tomb in Springfield. Regarding Eddie's...
home.att.net/~rjnorton/Lincoln67.htmlt
2. Tad Lincoln
...brothers, Eddie and Willie. Sources include Lincoln...child and as a teenager Thomas Lincoln ("Tad") was the fourth...
home.att.net/~rjnorton/Lincoln69.html
3. EWU Men's Basketball - November 10, 1999
...school seniors — Alvin Snow, Eddie Lincoln, Jeremy McCulloch and...Wash. (Franklin High School) Eddie Lincoln G/F - 6-5 - 195 -...
athletics.ewu.edu/99-00News/99mbnov10.htm
4. Abraham Lincoln Research Site
...FIRST SON Robert Lincoln THE LINCOLNS' SECOND SON Eddie...
Description: Aimed at families and students studying Abraham Lincoln's life, his family, his accomplish...
members.aol.com/RVSNorton/Lincoln2.html
5. Mary Todd Lincoln
...Kennedy, Mary Todd Lincoln was at her husband's side when an assassin...
Description: This site includes a biography, photographs, and other information about Mary Todd...
members.aol.com/RVSNorton/Lincoln15.html
6. Seattle Times: Metro League: Beach stops O'Dea...part of RB's 36 rebounds. Eddie Lincoln led the Irish with 24...
www.seattletimes.com/news/sports/html98/metr_20000205.html

7. Seattle Times: Metro League boys: Lincoln drives O'Dea victory

...Special to The Seattle Times Eddie Lincoln, the lone returning...Prep basket-ball Metro League boys: Lincoln drives O'Dea victory by Terry...

www.seattletimes.com/news/sports/html98/wood_19991204.html

8. best of the best game

...6'-9" 00 Pacific 149 Lincoln Eddie 6'-5" 00 O'Dea...have all the offers he'll get. Eddie Lincoln scored a bunch of...

www.socalhoops.com/prepnotes/0799/1bestpump710.htm

9. friends of hoop rosters

...(6'-8" Jr. C/F) Evergreen Eddie Lincoln (6'-5" Jr. F)...Aubry Shelton (6'-7" So. F/C) Lincoln FOH Black will play the True...

www.socalhoops.com/prepnotes/0499/foh0408.htm

10. Timeline of Lincoln's Life

....com/SunsetStrip/Venue/5217/eddie.html Eddie Lincoln site...of Abraham Lincoln's Life Year Date Event 1809 Feb 12 Son Abraham born to...

www.abrahamlincoln.cc/timeline.htm

•••

These results were not as good as Robert's results. "Eddie Lincoln" is a very common name, and Eddie Lincoln, the son of a president, was essentially irrelevant as an historical personality (compared to his older brother) because he died when he was only three years old. Therefore, the majority of results were about a high school basketball player named, yup, Eddie Lincoln.

We now move on to Lincoln son number three, Willie. The results:

1-10 results of about 89 for

"Willie Lincoln"

Search took 0.36 seconds.

1. Willie Lincoln

...Photograph) William Wallace Lincoln ("Willie") was born...of Abraham and Mary Todd Lincoln. Willie was named after Dr....

home.att.net/~rjnorton/Lincoln68.html - Cached - 10k - GoogleScout

2. Eddie Lincoln

...Edward Baker Lincoln, second son of Abraham and Mary Todd, was born March...Eddie was first published in 1998 in Lincoln's Photographs A Complete...

home.att.net/~rjnorton/Lincoln67.html

3. I9322: James John BOWIE (17 APR 1827 - 6 AUG 1871)

...Owen.Kardatzke@gsfc.nasa.gov William Wallace ("Willie") LINCOLN...___ |
|—William Wallace ("Willie") LINCOLN | |...

pickle.gsfc.nasa.gov/mdfams/D0006/G0000017.html

4. Willie Lincoln

... LINCOLN HOME NATIONAL HISTORIC SITE William "Willie" Wallace...child
of Mary and Abraham Lincoln, Willie, was born on December...

www.nps.gov/liho/family/willie.htm

5. I8625: William Wallace SEARS (21 APR 1828 -)

...on Thu Jul 25 12:39:15 1996 Willie Lincoln SEARS BIRTH: 25 JUN...| |
|_Jemima ROOT __ | |—Willie Lincoln SEARS | |...

www.genealogy.org/~lrsears/richard/d0012/g0001128.htm

6. Abraham Lincoln Research Site

...SECOND SON Eddie Lincoln THE LINCOLNS' THIRD SON Willie...

Description: Aimed at families and students studying Abraham Lincoln's life, his
family, his accomplish...

members.aol.com/RVSNorton/Lincoln2.html

7. Goats in the White House

...TAD AND WILLIE LINCOLN KEPT GOATS INSIDE THE WHITE HOUSE!
Gifts...the door again. Tad Lincoln and his father Willie Lincoln...

members.aol.com/RVSNorton/Lincoln33.html

8. Connie Willis, IL SOGNO DI LINCOLN, (Lincoln's Dream, 1987),...di Lincoln
fossero dovuti alla morte del figlioletto Willie (II...,prima sepoltura del piccolo
Willie Lincoln. Al tempo stesso, egli...

www.intercom.publinet.it/1999/lincoln.htm

9. Abraham Lincoln and Animals

...to the executioner. Tad and Willie Lincoln Kept Goats inside the...Young Tad
Lincoln Saved the Life of Jack, the White House Turkey Late in...

www.iaa-online.org/Lincoln.htm

10. timeline.htm

...Springfield 1850 - Edward Lincoln died 1850 - Willie...President 1861 - Lincoln
gave 1st inaugural address 1862 - Willie...

www.mmtcnet.com/dterich/lincoln/timeline.htm

•••

These results are more on-target, although we are beginning to see
some unavoidable duplication of results from Robert's findings. Nevertheless, we can now plunder a few more sites that appear to be of some
value for our task. We conclude with a search for information about the
Lincolns' youngest boy, Tad. The results:

1-10 results of about 128 for

"Tad Lincoln"

Search took 0.49 seconds.

1. Tad Lincoln

...Tad as a very young child and as a teenager Thomas Lincoln...on April 4, 1853. Tad was named after Thomas Lincoln, Abraham's...

home.att.net/~rjnorton/Lincoln69.html

2. Tad Lincoln

www.historybuff.com/library/reftad.html

3. Tad Lincoln

...Tad Lincoln: The Not-so-Famous Son of A Most-Famous President By...delving into the life of Tad (Theodore) Lincoln. What I discovered...

www.historybuff.com/library/reftad.html

4. CARTE DE VISITE - Thomas "Tad" Lincoln

...impulsive personality, Tad became the focus of Lincoln's...William Wallace in 1862. Tad died in 1871. Of Lincoln's four sons,...

www.npg.si.edu/exh/brady/gallery/96gal.html

5. Lieutenant Tad Lincoln's Sentinels

...Lieutenant Tad Lincoln's Sentinels President Lincoln's...quarters...His brother objected but Tad insisted upon his rights as an...

www.acclaimedmedia.com/voafa/lincoln/144.htm

6. Tad Lincoln Saves Jack

...YOUNG TAD LINCOLN SAVED THE LIFE OF JACK, THE WHITE HOUSE TURKEY!...for the Lincoln family to feast on during the holidays. Tad...

members.aol.com/RVSNorton1/Lincoln65.html

7. Abraham Lincoln Research Site

...THIRD SON Willie Lincoln THE LINCOLNS' FOURTH SON Tad...

Description: Aimed at families and students studying Abraham

Lincoln's life, his family, his accomplish...

members.aol.com/RVSNorton/Lincoln2.html

8. I22698: Joseph ELLIOT (22 MAY 1740 -)

...Owen.Kardatzke@gsfc.nasa.gov Thomas ("Tad") LINCOLN Birth: 4 APR...I_?daughter BERRY ___ I I—Thomas ("Tad") LINCOLN I I...

pickle.gsfc.nasa.gov/mdfams/D0005/G0000017.html

9. Tad Lincoln

... LINCOLN HOME NATIONAL HISTORIC SITE Thomas (Tad) Lincoln...after Lincoln's father, Thomas, but, Abraham nicknamed him "Tad,"...

www.nps.gov/liho/family/tad.htm

10. The Missouri Review: Fiction, Poetry, Nonfiction, Features, and Interviews...Guestbook Discussion E-Mail Tad Lincoln's Ladder of Dreams by...on

the floor to button me up. Tad Lincoln, they said: look at how...
www.missourireview.org/fiction/pease.html

Eight of these 10 sites are directly concerned with Tad Lincoln and should prove worthwhile to peruse. Since Tad Lincoln is also a fairly common name, it is not surprising that a couple of unrelated sites popped up in the search. Regardless of that, we now have dozens of Web sites to review for information about Lincoln's son.

Barnes & Noble Online (bn.com)

From here, I went on to a search for useful books about our subject. I began with a search of *bn.com*. I began with a general search for Abraham Lincoln-related titles. The results:

There are 342 matching titles.
1 - 10 below in bestselling order.
1. Lincoln as I Knew Him: Gossip, Tributes and Revelations from his Best Friends and Worst Enemies
Harold Holzer (Editor)
Hardcover / Algonquin Books of Chapel Hill / October 1999
Our Price: $11.86, You Save 30%
2. Abe Lincoln's Hat (Step into Reading Books Series: A Step 2 Book)
Martha Brenner, Donald Cook (Illustrator)
Paperback / Random House / March 1994
Our Price: $3.19, You Save 20%
3. Abraham Lincoln: Great Emancipator (The Childhood of Famous Americans Series)
Augusta Stevenson, Jerry Robinson (Illustrator)
Paperback / Simon & Schuster Children's / August 1982
Our Price: $3.99, You Save 20%
4. Meet Abraham Lincoln
Barbara Cary,Stephen Marchesi
Paperback / Random House Books for Young Readers / April 1989
Our Price: $3.19, You Save 20%
5. Abraham Lincoln: Redeemer President
Allen C. Guelzo
Hardcover / William B. Eerdmans Publishing Co. / September 1999

Our Price: $20.30, You Save 30%

6. A Picture Book of Abraham Lincoln

David A. Adler, Alexandra Wallner (Illustrator), John C. Wallner (Illustrator)

Paperback / Holiday House, Inc. / February 1990

Our Price: $5.56, You Save 20%

7. Lincoln

David Herbert Donald

Paperback / Simon & Schuster Trade / October 1996

Our Price: $13.60, You Save 20%

8. An Acquaintance with Darkness

Ann Rinaldi

Mass Market Paperback / Harcourt Brace & Company / April 1999

Our Price: $4.80, You Save 20%

9. Abe: A Novel about Abraham Lincoln's Youth

Richard Slotkin

Hardcover / Henry Holt & Company / January 2000

Our Price: $19.25, You Save 30%

10. Reelecting Lincoln: The Battle for the 1864 Presidency

John C. Waugh

Hardcover / Crown Publishing Group / January 1998

Our Price: $6.98, You Save 76%

•••

Of these top 10 books, *Lincoln As I Knew Him* might contain some anecdotes about Lincoln's sons. The David Donald biography might be worth checking out (he's an acclaimed Lincoln authority). I was able to immediately recognize David Donald's name because, as we discussed earlier, his name was often cited in other materials I dug up while researching Lincoln's life and I made a point of keeping an eye out for works and writings by Donald for further study. This confluence of names and sources will happen with almost any subject you research.

I then searched Barnes & Noble for "Lincoln's sons" and "Abraham Lincoln AND sons" and each time two titles came back. One was a completely unrelated book written in German, and the other was a book called *Sculptor's Son*, which was about Lincoln Borglum, the sculptor of Mount Rushmore. Aside from the interesting synchronicity of Lincoln being on

Mount Rushmore and the juxtaposition of the words "son" and the sculptor's first name, neither of these books would likely be of any use to us. (Although this is one of those nuggets of information I would file away for later use as a colorful anecdote in my Lincoln projects. This is one of those factoids that inevitably elicits a "Who knew?" response from someone you tell it to.)

Bibliofind.com (used and out-of-print books)

Then, I traveled into the world of used and out-of-print books. Our first stop...*Bibliofind.com.*

I searched for books about Lincoln on Bibliofind using the search term "Lincoln" and got back several pages of used and out-of-print books. The following list is the first 50 or so titles. As you can see, based on their titles, none of them are really much help for information about Lincoln's sons. Some of them look to be promising as secondary sources, especially the biography of Mary Todd Lincoln, and some of the multivolume biographies.

I've included this list of titles to also illustrate how a search can go wrong. Notice the titles that are completely irrelevant to our search for Lincoln information (19, 21, 37). However, these came up because the title had the word "Lincoln" in it. This is why you must be specific with your search terms. (And before you ask, I haven't a clue how *Narratives Of The Indian Wars, 1675-1699* came back from a search for "Lincoln!")

1. Abe Lincoln In Illinois: A Play in Twelve Scenes
2. Abraham Lincoln (6 different books with this title)
3. Abraham Lincoln (With First Publication of the Speech Delivered by Lincoln in New York, February 27, 1860)
4. Abraham Lincoln as a Man of Letters
5. Abraham Lincoln Heroes and Leaders in American History
6. Abraham Lincoln in Six Volumes
7. Abraham Lincoln, Man of God
8. Abraham Lincoln Nation's Leader in the Great Struggle Through Which Was Maintained the Existence of the United States
9. Abraham Lincoln Prairie Years
10. Abraham Lincoln War Years

11. Abraham Lincoln: The People's Leader in the Struggle for National Existence

12. Abraham Lincoln: A New Portrait

13. Abraham Lincoln: A Poem

14. Abraham Lincoln: An Initial Biography

15. The Apprenticeship of Abraham Lincoln

16. Arrival 12:30: The Baltimore Plot Against Lincoln

17. The Cathedral Church of Lincoln

18. Conversations With Lincoln

19. The Dane: A Legend of Old Grimsby and Lincoln

20. The Emergence of Lincoln

21. Full Particulars of the Life and Dying Moments of William Longland, Executed on the New Drop, Lincoln, for Aiding, Counselling, and Being Accessary to Burglary at Grantham; Lincoln

22. Gettysburg and Lincoln: The Battle, The Cemetery, and The National Park

23. Narratives Of The Indian Wars, 1675-1699

24. If Lincoln Were Here

25. The Life of Abraham Lincoln

26. Lincoln (2 different books with this title)

27. Lincoln and His Cabinet

28. The Lincoln Centennial Medal

29. Lincoln Frees the Slaves

30. Lincoln Goes Around the World

31. Lincoln Image: Abraham Lincoln and the Popular Print

32. The Lincoln Tribute Book

33. Lincoln: A Psycho-Biography

34. Lincoln: An Illustrated Biography

35. A Man Named Lincoln

36. A Memorial for Mr. Lincoln

37. Notes on the Monasteries and Other Religious Institutions Near the River Witham, From Lincoln to the Sea

38. Personal Recollections of Abraham Lincoln

39. The Political Debates Between Abraham Lincoln and Stephen A. Douglas

40. The Presidents Wife: Mary Todd Lincoln

41. The Publications of the Lincoln Record Society

42. Six Hundred Questions About Lincoln—How Many Can You Answer?

43. The Statesmanship of Abraham Lincoln

44. The Story of Lincoln Minster

45. The Voice of Lincoln
46. The War for the Union
47. Washington and Lincoln
48. The Writings of Abraham Lincoln
49. The Writings of Abraham Lincoln Constitutional Edition (Volume 5 Of 8)
50. The Writings of Abraham Lincoln With an Introduction by Theodore Roosevelt

•••

After these results I conducted a new search, but this time, my title search term was "Lincoln's Sons." Bingo! Bibliofind returned 46 titles, 45 of which were Ruth Painter's masterful biography *Lincoln's Sons*. The books available ranged in price from $4 to 10 times that. (I bought the one offered for $4.) The 46th title was a book called *Lincoln's Camera Man: Mathew B. Brady*. Why did this one show up? Because it was published by Scribner's Sons and the word "Lincoln" and "Sons" were both in the "title" field in the Bibliofind database and so it registered as a positive result. This should serve to make you more aware of the incredible power—and incredible stupidity—of search engines and other Web scouring tools: To a search engine, the word "sons" is the word "sons," and, thus, the false return. This is not the search engine's fault; it was mine for not adding restrictive qualifier terms and further narrowing my search.

Lincoln periodicals

As part of my research process, in addition to books and Web sites, I always also look for journals, magazines, and other periodical publications that might contain useful information related to my search. With this in mind, I returned to *iWon.com* and did a search using the search term "Lincoln journals."

Many of the results were useless, and included newsletters published by towns named Lincoln, and other ephemera unrelated to our expedition for information about the sons of Mary and Abraham Lincoln.

One search result did look promising, though. It was titled "Abraham Lincoln Periodicals" and when I clicked through I came upon the following list:

Abraham Lincoln Periodicals
The Journal of the Abraham Lincoln Association
Journals Department
University of Illinois Press
1325 S. Oak Street
Champaign, IL 61820-6903

Lincoln Legal Briefs
The Lincoln Legal Papers
1 Old State Capitol Plaza
Springfield, IL 62701-1507
(217)785-9130
FAX: (217)524-6973
E-mail: *LLP@uis.edu*

Lincoln Herald
Lincoln Memorial University
Harrogate, TN 37752

Lincoln Lore
The Lincoln Museum
200 E. Berry
P.O. Box 7838
Fort Wayne, IN 46801-7838

Illinois Historical Journal
Historic Preservation Agency
Old State Capitol
Springfield, IL 62701

Surratt House Courier
Surratt House Museum
9118 Brandywine Road
Clinton, Maryland 20735
(301)868-1121

The Lincoln Newsletter
Lincoln College
Lincoln, IL 62565
The Lincoln Ledger
Lincoln Fellowship of Wisconsin
1923 Grange Avenue
Racine, WI 53403-2328

The Lincolnian
Lincoln Group of the District of Columbia
7415 Flora Street
Springfield, VA 22150

Journal of the Lincoln Assassination
Autograph Press
P.O. Box 380545
San Antonio, TX 78280

The Rail Splitter
(For Dealers and Collectors)
Box 275
New York, NY 10044
Phone: (212)980-7031
Fax: (212)741-8756

Wow, could I be so lucky? Yes, I could...thanks to the awesome power of the Internet. This search had returned a complete list, with contact information, of almost a dozen journals and magazines devoted solely to Lincoln and "Lincolniana."

In addition, several of these titles were underlined as clickable links (URLs) which took me right to the Web page of the journals. In the Immersion step of my research process, these types of leads are invaluable. If I was actually giving the speech, or writing the book, paper, or article about Lincoln's sons, I would go to each one of these clickable sites and search for the sons by name, or review the journal's index if it did not offer search capabilities on its site.

For the journals that did not offer Web access, I don't think I would write to them. That would probably take too long. In addition, it is possible (if not likely) that my query letter might get lost or buried under a pile of incoming correspondence. (This I know from firsthand experience.) Instead, I would probably call the mags and speak to one of the editors or the librarian of the journal (if there was one) to describe my project to them. Hopefully, this would result in either a "Yes, we have a great deal of information that might help you," "Sorry, we don't have anything that can help you," or something in between. In any case, I would be one more step down the road towards accumulating as much information as possible before I started the note-taking process.

The Reader's Guide to Periodical Literature

The Reader's Guide to Periodical Literature is an annual compilation of articles organized by subject that were published in magazines during the previous year. It is considered by many to be the gold standard when it comes to the indexing of periodical articles. Every library stocks it and it goes back to the 1890s.

For the purposes of our four hypothetical "Lincoln's sons" projects, I reviewed the *Reader's Guide* from 1890 (the earliest edition of the publication) through 1935 (after Robert Todd Lincoln's death) to find pertinent articles related to Lincoln and his sons.

As you might suspect, the articles about Abraham Lincoln were voluminous. However, those about his wife and sons were not so plentiful. The first volume in the series spans 1890 through 1899 and listed 94 articles about Lincoln, organized into the following 17 categories:

- General (13 articles).
- About (34 articles).
- Anecdotes (4 articles).
- As a lawyer (5 articles).
- Assassination (5 articles).
- Biography (3 articles).
- Cartoon, satire, etc. (1 article).
- Election (3 articles).
- Family (1 article).
- Fiction (1 article).
- Literary art (3 articles).
- Memorial services (1 article).
- Monuments, etc. (1 article).
- Poems about (16 articles).
- Political career before 1861 (1 article).
- Relics (1 article).
- Views on slavery (1 article).

There was also a separate listing for "Lincoln, Mary (Todd) (Mrs. Abraham Lincoln)" (1 article); and "Lincoln, Robert Todd" (1 article). This was a consistent trend throughout *Reader's Guide* listings for Mary Todd Lincoln and Robert Todd Lincoln. There were always dozens for Abraham Lincoln but two or three for his wife and eldest son...at the most. There were hardly any articles listed for Lincoln's other three sons.

I continued my research by reviewing the citations listings from the other nine selected volumes of the *Reader's Guide*:

- 1890 to 1899 (94 articles).
- 1900 to 1904 (41 articles).
- 1905 to 1909 (169 articles).
- 1910 to 1914 (85 articles).
- 1915 to 1918 (85 articles).
- 1919 to 1921 (71 articles).
- 1922 to 1924 (55 articles).
- 1925 to 1928 (94 articles).
- January 1929 to June 1932 (68 articles).
- July 1932 to June 1935 (50 articles).

Here is a look at a sample citation listing from the *Reader's Guide* from the 1890-1899 "Family" heading for Abraham Lincoln:

Chittenden, L. E. Genealogy of Abraham Lincoln. Harp W
40:182 F 22 '96

Translated, this means that an article titled "Genealogy of Abraham Lincoln" by L. E. Chittenden was published in volume 40, on page 182 of *Harper's Weekly* on February 22, 1896.

If I were actually writing our four works, I would review the titles of every one of the 812 articles cited and make a master list of those I wanted to look at. I would then have to compare my "want list" with the library's holdings (their periodicals archives). I would probably be able to get my hands on copies of most of what I wanted to read. Many university libraries and larger libraries have microfilm and microfiche archives of a great many periodicals dating back to the turn of the century. By simply knowing what you want to see (the February 22, 1896 issue of *Harper's Weekly* from our citation above), you can easily access information that can be invaluable for your individual project.

The card catalog

During my university library visit, I also consulted the card catalog for Lincoln titles and Lincoln-related titles. Before I discuss what I found, I think a word is in order here about the two types of classification systems used in libraries. The two types used are the **Dewey Decimal System** and the **Library of Congress (LOC) Classification System**. The Library of Congress System is used in most larger public libraries and in all university libraries. The Dewey Decimal System is used in most smaller libraries.

The Dewey Decimal System

The Dewey Decimal System is a numeric classification system that groups nonfiction books into 10 categories:

- 000-099 General works, encyclopedias
- 100-199 Philosophy
- 200-299 Religion
- 300-399 Social sciences
- 400-499 Language
- 500-599 Pure science
- 600-699 Technology
- 700-799 Arts
- 800-899 Literature
- 900-999 History

For our Lincoln research, it would be a pretty safe bet that the books that would be the most useful to us would be found in the 900-999 category (history) and maybe the 300-399 category (Social Sciences) as that category also includes works about government that could hold something of interest.

The Library of Congress Classification System

The Library of Congress Classification System is an alphanumeric classification system that groups nonfiction books into 21 classes:

A   General works
B   Philosophy, psychology, and religion
C   Auxiliary sciences of history
D   History: general and outside the Americas
E   History: America (general) and United States (general)
F   History: United States (local), Canada, Central and South America, the Caribbean
G   Geography, anthropology, recreation
H   Social sciences
J   Political science
K   Law
L   Education
M   Music
N   Fine arts
P   Language and literature
Q   Science
R   Medicine
S   Agriculture
T   Technology
U   Military science
V   Naval science
Z   Bibliography and library science

Again, for our Lincoln research, we would look to the D and E categories, although the card catalog would steer you to the right category by the information each card used to identify a book.

I found a sought-after biography of Robert Todd Lincoln at my university library during a search through the card catalog and, sure enough, its LOC number was:

E
664
L63
G6

This not only told me where to find the book in the library, but also that it was classified under general American history.

For your specific book, article, speech, or term paper research, it would be helpful for you to identify the category in both classification systems in which books relevant to your topic will be found. For example, I found a 71 titles related to Lincoln, his wife, and his sons, including the Robert Todd Lincoln biography previously mentioned.

These "Looking for Lincolns" examples demonstrate the procedures for research you need to do on the Internet, and at one or more libraries to accumulate relevant materials for your Immersion.

appendix

Suggested Web Sites for Research

ometimes we can have so many bookmarks stored on our browser that we end up ignoring all of them and instead going to the Web to find what we need. Admit it: This has happened to you, right? It seems as though Henry David Thoreau's timeless exhortation to simplify should also apply to our bookmarks list.

To prevent this kind of aimless wandering, here is a streamlined list of search engines, reference sites, and book retailers that should be more than adequate for almost all your research needs.

If one of these sites can't find you what you want, do what you want, or take you where you want to go, then you can always start clicking through links. But for most of your needs, these should be plenty.

Search engines

www.google.com

- Super-fast search engine; highly recommended. Has won awards for its streamlined, highly efficient functionality.

www.raging.com

- Another stripped-down, super-fast search engine; also highly recommended.

www.altavista.com

- One of the big boys; a multifunction portal, but it might be a tad slow.

www.excite.com

- Good all-purpose search engine.

www.northernlight.com

- A good all-purpose search engine that groups categories in separate folders.

www.infoseek.com

- Good all-purpose search engine that allows you to search within a set of results, refining your search terms until you find the most relevant sites. When you need to start with a very broad topic and then narrow it down until it's what you are looking for, Infoseek cannot be beat.

www.dogpile.com

- Dogpile performs a Web search with several search engines at the same time and returns results by Web site. I like to use Dogpile for when I want to do a wide-ranging search utilizing the different search protocols of several search engines.

www.ask.com

- A search engine that allows you to search using plain language questions, such as, "Where can I find information about the Renaissance painter Giotto?" Sometimes the results can be bizarre, but it uses several search engines at once and can usually steer you to sites that contain the answer to your question.

www.infojump.com
- A search engine for 5,000,000 full-text magazine and newspaper articles, but results can be odd sometimes.

Books

Amazon.com
- Perhaps one of the best sources on the Web for finding salient information about all things bookish.

www.bn.com **(Barnes & Noble)**
- The bookseller's site; good for buying books, of course, but also for finding out what's currently in print. There are many other book sites on the Web, but all you really need is one: *bn.com.*

www.bibliofind.com **(Bibliofind)** or *www.abe.com* **(abebooks)**
- Bibliofind is one of the best used and out-of-print book search services on the Web, in my opinion, and it will hook you up with scads of used book dealers all over the country. Its search engine is fast and accurate, and extremely easy to use. Also, abebooks is equally good. Between these two services, if a used book exists, you should be able to find it.

promo.net/pg/ **(Project Gutenberg)**
- Project Gutenberg offers thousands of **free, public domain** books for downloading plain text documents. Books are constantly being added to the site and the downloads are quick and reliable. The last time I visited Project Gutenberg, there were close to 2,800 titles being offered, including works by Edgar Allan Poe, Spinoza, Shakespeare (the complete works), Jack London, Luther, Goethe, and George Bernard Shaw; as well as things like *The First 100,000 Prime Numbers*, Buddhist tracts, and complete issues of *Popular Science Monthly* from 1915. Project Gutenberg is a gold mine of material for the scholar, writer, researcher, and just plain reader; but it is also a public service of the highest magnitude, making public domain books available on the Internet for free.

Reference

www.britannica.com

- *The Encyclopedia Britannica*, the classic encyclopedia, now online.

www.fathom.com

- A joint partnership of Columbia University, London School of Economics and Political Science, the British Library, Cambridge University Press, the Smithsonian Institution, and the New York Public Library, this new site (as of fall 2000) is a definitive and authoritative information portal. Most preliminary information on a subject is free, but charges will be levied as users move into deeper content.

www.fedworld.gov

- Federal documents...perhaps *all* of them, (although probably not).

www.encyclopedia.com

- The online version of the Concise Columbia Encyclopedia.

www.whowhere.lycos.com

- A massive resource for phone numbers, street addresses, and e-mail addresses.

www.onelook.com

- A dictionary search service that utilizes 500 dictionaries to look up your word.

www.biography.com

- 20,000 short biographies. Good for basic biographical information to get you started.

babelfish.altavista.com

- A translation site that allows you to type in text in several different languages and then choose into which of several languages you would like the text translated. You can also type in the URL of a Web site and tell the site what language to translate your target site into, while retaining the original layout and graphics. You may not ever need this site, but when and if you do, it's nice to know it's there waiting for you.

A caution, though. Sometimes the translation results are less than accurate. I had this site translate an interview I did with an Italian magazine. I responded to the interview questions in English, the editor translated my words into Italian, and I used *babelfish.altavista.com* to translate it back into English. Yikes. The gist of my responses came through, but *serious* editing would have been necessary to transform the translation into publishable form.

vancouver-Webpages.com/wordnet/index.html

- An excellent online thesaurus.

www.writeexpress.com/online.html

- A very complete rhyming dictionary for poets and songwriters.

www.usps.gov/ncsc/lookups/lookup_ctystzip.html

- Find a ZIP code by city or find a city by ZIP code.

www.geocities.com/wallstreet/exchange/1161/index.htm

- A listing of worldwide postal rates.

www.acronymfinder.com

- A comprehensive acronym finder that also allows you to do a reverse lookup by a keyword search.

www.lexis-nexis.com

- A legal, news, and business information service that provides access to over 73,000 databases and over 1 billion documents...but it's not free. Sometimes libraries subscribe and allow patrons to use the service for a limited time. You can also subscribe at home. Nonsubscribers can access "Lexis-Nexis Express" for a one-time fee.

39 Reference Works for Research and Writing

> ❝ *Everyone knows that in research there are no final answers, only insights that allow one to formulate new questions.* ❞
>
> —**Salvador Luria**

You've hit the Web sites. You've been to the library. You've plundered the *Reader's Guide.* You've bought subject-specific books about your topic. You may have even called a few experts to ask some relevant questions. But if you have plans on writing more than the one piece you have been working on while reading this book, all of that is not enough.

Every writer—be it of fiction or nonfiction—needs a basic library of reference works within arm's reach. This includes—but is not limited to—a dictionary (or six—I recommend *Webster's* and the *Illustrated Oxford*), a thesaurus (several), a couple of books of quotations (or more), an atlas, and many books on the rules of grammar.

The nonfiction writer, however, needs a considerably more varied collection of reference books, because the nonfiction writer's job is fact-laden and detail-intense.

The nonfiction writer may, depending on the project at hand, instantly need answers to questions, such as "Who wrote the song 'Hatari!'?"

(Henry Mancini), "What is the official language of Uganda?" (English), "What do you call a baby rhinoceros?" (a calf), "Who discovered benzene?" (Michael Faraday), and "Is it true that masturbation is illegal in Michigan?" (yes, it is punishable by a fine and five years in jail).

In the almost three decades that I have been writing nonfiction, I have assembled an enormous library of nonfiction books that I have turned to on many occasions for answers to an eclectic range of questions. Some books I have purchased as soon as they were published at retail prices, including books on the Titanic, a book of Presidential quotations, and a memoir by a funeral director.

I have bought many books at remainder book warehouses simply because they looked interesting (and they were so cheap I couldn't resist). These fortuitous finds have often been some of my most valuable resources. Some of these books include a huge *Rolling Stone Album Guide*; a UFO encyclopedia; several video guides; several American History reference books; Civil War dictionaries, atlases, and encyclopedias; a dictionary of cliches, a dictionary of slang, medical books, art books, books of quotations; rare, out-of-print biographies, and much more.

Here is a list of 39 nonfiction reference works that, in addition to the dictionaries and thesauri mentioned above, should prove useful in answering all manner of intriguing questions.

The freelancer's bible

Writer's Market (Writer's Digest Books, annual). See Chapter 22 for more about this valuable resource. You should buy this yearly if you do a lot of freelancing or plan to do a lot of submitting.

The King James Bible

Regardless of your religious persuasion, a copy of the Bible is a must for every writer. The lyrical use of language in the Good Book can inspire your own work, plus the references to the Bible running throughout literature and film will undoubtedly prove enlightening.

"Physician, heal thyself" is from the Gospel of Luke. Abraham Lincoln drew the theme for his "House Divided" speech from the Gospel of

Mark: "If a house be divided against itself, that house cannot stand." The title of the film *Tender Mercies* is from the Book of Proverbs: "A righteous man regardeth the life of his beast, but the tender mercies of the wicked are cruel." The instances of the Bible being used as a source for literary and cinematic references is almost endless. Refer to it often for ideas and to immerse yourself in its beautifully written stories.

8 quotations books

A writer can never have too many quotations books. They not only provide a plethora of pithy quotes to use in your text and as epigraphs, they also can aid in your research by revealing the source of a saying or an adage you would like to refer to, but need to know the author and the work first. Many quotations dictionaries are indexed by keyword, allowing you to quickly hone in on your topic. For example, 50 quotations with the word "marriage" in them. There are also many quotations Web sites, but here are eight titles you will undoubtedly find extremely useful…and will want to own:

- *The Oxford Dictionary of Quotations* (Oxford University Press, 1979).
- *The Oxford Dictionary of Modern Quotations* (Oxford University Press, 1991).
- *The New York Public Library Book of 20th-Century American Quotations* (Warner Books, 1992).
- *The Great Quotations* (Pocket Books, 1967).
- *Instant Quotation Dictionary* (Dell, 1972).
- *Bartlett's Familiar Quotations: A Collection of Passages, Phrases, and Proverbs Traced to Their Sources in Ancient and Modern Literature, 9th edition* (Little, Brown, 1901).
- *Friendly Advice: A Compendium of Wise, Witty and Irreverent Counsel* compiled and edited by Jon Winokur (Dutton, 1990).
- *The World Almanac of Presidential Quotations* (Pharos Books, 1988).

3 books on grammar and style

These kinds of books are important to have around for when you are not sure if you are violating some rule of grammar, or if you need clarification on literary techniques and styles. You probably won't refer to these books on a daily basis, but when you need them, you need them.

- *The Elements of Style* by William Strunk Jr. and E. B. White (Allyn & Bacon, 1999).
- *A Dictionary of Modern English Usage* (Oxford University Press, 1997).
- *Essentials of English: A Practical Handbook of Grammar and Effective Writing Techniques* (Barron's, 1990).
- *On Writing: A Memoir of the Craft* by Stephen King (Scribner's, 2000).

The New York Public Library series

- *The New York Public Library Desk Reference* (Macmillan, 1998). This valuable reference is similar in scope and intent to the *World Almanac* but provides more in-depth information, with detailed essays and articles about a wide range of topics. The book is organized into six main sections: "The Physical World," "The World of Ideas," "The Way We Communicate," "Daily Life," "Recreation," and "The Political World," with many subtopics covered for each main section. Invaluable.
- *The New York Public Library Book of How and Where To Look It Up* (Macmillan, 1991). This bills itself as "the ultimate one-volume reference guide to the best, most up-to-date and readily available resources." Useful.
- *The New York Public Library American History Desk Reference* (Macmillan, 1997). The New York Public Library does it again, but this time the focus is on American History. An excellent, one-volume resource—very well-organized.
- *The New York Public Library Book of Popular Americana* (Macmillan, 1994). An A-to Z of American popular

culture, including fads, catch phrases, sports figures, slogans, popular singers, political leaders, and much, much more.

3 books about words

- *The Superior Person's Book of Words* by Peter Bowler (Laureleaf, 1990).
- *The Dictionary of Cliches* by James Rogers (Ballantine, 1987).
- *Slang and Euphemism: A Dictionary of Oaths, Curses, Insults, Sexual Slang and Metaphor, Racial Slurs, Drug Talk, Homosexual Lingo, and Related Matters* by Richard A. Spears (Signet, 1991). A classic.

Miscellaneous reference books

- *The World Almanac and Book of Facts* (distributed by St. Martin's Press, annual). This annual goldmine of facts contains an almost surreal amount of valuable information and can probably answer a huge number of factual questions instantly. A must for every writer's office (and yes, you should buy a new one each year).
- *The People's Chronology* by James Trager (Henry Holt, 1994) This amazing 1,237-page, million-plus word volume bills itself as "A Year-by-Year Record of Human Events from Prehistory to the Present" and it means it. I make use of this book on a regular basis and am eagerly awaiting the next edition. The 1992 edition ends with events in 1991 and is now out of print. It is worth trying to find as a used copy, however, and I quickly found reasonably priced copies of both the original 1979 edition and the 1992 edition on Bibliofind (*bibliofind.com*). We can only hope that Trager is working on a new edition to be published in 2002.
- *The Guinness Book of World Records* (Guinness Publishing, annual). You may not need a new copy every year, but this book should be in the library of every writer. I am not exaggerating when I say that there are at least a dozen fantastic story or book ideas on every page of this book. For example, on page 9 of the

1998 edition there are blurbs about the world's longest pencil, the world's biggest pinata, the world's tallest snowman, the world's longest zipper, the world's most complex Rube Goldberg machine, and the world's largest Santa Claus. There. I now have ideas for my next six magazine articles or books.

- ***The Timeline Book of Science: A Lively and Completely Comprehensive View of Science and Technology, from the Discovery of Fire to the Advent of the Electronic Age***
  and
- ***The Timeline Book of the Arts: A Lively and Completely Comprehensive View of the Creative Arts, from the First Cave Paintings to Today's Top Movies and TV Programs*** both by George Ochoa and Melinda Corey (Ballantine, 1995) Excellent references in an easy-to-use, chronologically formatted index.

- ***The Complete Book of U. S. Presidents, 4th Edition*** by William A. DeGregorio (Barricade Books, 1993) For your money, this is the best, single-volume reference on American presidents.

- ***The Oxford Companion to American Military History*** (Oxford University Press, 1999). A massive volume containing over 1,000 alphabetical entries about American military history, from "ABM Treaty" to "Elmo R. Zumwalt, Jr." This book weighs in at over a million words and contains lengthy, authoritative essays and articles by more than 500 of the world's most acclaimed historians, academics, researchers and writers.

- ***The Bantam Medical Dictionary*** (Bantam, 1982). A comprehensive dictionary comprised of 9,500 alphabetical entries that will allow you to use "aortic stenosis" correctly in a sentence (assuming, of course, that the occasion arises where you will *need* to use it correctly). Seriously, though, a good medical dictionary is a necessary part of every nonfiction writer's library.

- ***The Encyclopedia of Mammals*** by Dr. David W. Macdonald (Checkmark Books, 1995). A huge volume covering mammals from carnivores to marsupials. (And yes, in case you were wondering, odd-toed ungulates are covered in detail.)

- ***Merriam-Webster's Encyclopedia of Literature*** (Merriam-Webster, 1995). An absolutely unbeatable one-volume encyclopedia of writers, works, literary terms and topics from all eras and all parts of the world. This tome insightfully covers literary works, classic authors of the past, well-known authors of today, mythological figures, fictional characters, literary terms, literary styles and movements, scholars and critics, and literary landmarks, prizes, and journals.

- ***The Whole Pop Catalog: The Berkeley Pop Culture Project*** (Avon, 1991). A fascinating, extensively illustrated, exhaustively researched encyclopedia of popular culture—from Abbott and Costello and advertising, to wrestling and yo-yos.

- ***Who Wrote That Song?*** by Dick Jacobs and Harriet Jacobs (Writer's Digest Books, 1994) Tells you who wrote the music and words to more than 12,500 popular American songs, including when each song was published, who popularized it, and more. Invaluable when you need to know the composer of an obscure song or the popularizer of a song from a long-forgotten Broadway musical. The book also contains an index of songwriters, allowing you to see, at a glance, everything hundreds of songwriters wrote; plus lists of Grammy Awards, Academy Awards, and much more.

- ***Videohound's Golden Movie Retriever*** (Visible Ink, annual) A ridiculously complete movie encyclopedia, including detailed reviews of over 24,000 movies, with indexes that cross-reference directors, actors, screenwriters, composers, and more. This book will probably answer any question you may have about the movies. If it does not, then you can hit the Internet Movie Database (*www.imdb.com*) on the Web, but this volume could save a log-on. What's that? You want to know what was Zasu Pitts's first movie? *Greed*, 1924. Her last? *It's a Mad, Mad, Mad World*, 1963. Who directed *Greed*, you ask? Erich von Stroheim.

- ***Final Curtain*** by Everett G. Jarvis (Citadel Press, 1998). A massive directory of celebrity birth and death dates, including causes of death and where each celeb is buried. Want to know which celebrities died from AIDS? Heart failure? Suicide? It's all in here, conveniently indexed and cross-referenced. Morbid? A little. But as I have repeatedly said, when you need to know something that is chronicled in this book, you'll be thankful you have it at hand.

- ***The Complete Directory to Prime Time Network and Cable TV Shows, 1946-Present*** by Tim Brooks and Earle Marsh (Ballantine, 1999). *TV Guide* calls this book "the *Encyclopedia Britannica* of television" and *TV Guide* oughta know, right?

Internet guides

- ***The Internet Handbook for Writers, Researchers, and Journalists*** by Mary McGuire, Linda Stilborne, Melinda McAdams, Laurel Hyatt (The Guilford Press, 2000).
- ***The Internet: The Rough Guide*** by Angus J. Kennedy (distributed by Penguin, 1999).
- ***Researching Online for Dummies, 2nd Edition*** by Reva Basch (IDG Books, 1998).
- ***Internet Directory for Dummies*** by Brad Hill (IDG Books, 1998).
- ***The Internet for Dummies, 5th Edition*** by John Levine, Carol Baroudi, Margaret Levine Young (IDG Books, 1998).

Index

W

About the Author

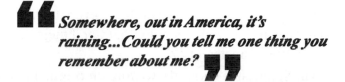 *Somewhere, out in America, it's raining... Could you tell me one thing you remember about me?*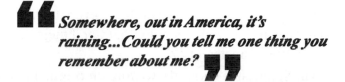

"Have You Seen Me Lately?"
—Counting Crows

**tephen J. Spignesi** is a full-time writer who specializes in nonfiction popular culture and historical subjects, including historical biography, television, film, American history, and contemporary fiction.

Mr. Spignesi (dubbed "the world's leading authority on Stephen King" by *Entertainment Weekly* magazine) has written many authorized entertainment books and has worked with Stephen King, Turner Entertainment, the Margaret Mitchell Estate, Andy Griffith, Viacom, and other entertainment industry personalities and entities on a wide range of projects. Mr. Spignesi has also contributed essays, chapters, articles, and introductions to many books.

Mr. Spignesi's books have been translated into several languages and he has also written for *Harper's*, *Cinefantastique*, *Saturday Review*, *Mystery Scene*, *Gauntlet*, and *Midnight Graffiti* magazines, as well as *The New York Times*, the New York *Daily News*, the *New York Post*, *The New Haven Register*, the French literary journal *Ténébres* and the Italian online literary journal, *Horror.It*. Mr. Spignesi

has also appeared on CNN, MSNBC, Fox News Channel, and other TV and radio outlets, and also appeared in the 1998 E! documentary, "The Kennedys: Power, Seduction, and Hollywood," as a Kennedy family authority; and in the A & E *Biography* of Stephen King that aired in January 2000. Mr. Spignesi's 1997 book *JFK Jr.* was a *New York Times* best-seller.

In addition to writing, Mr. Spignesi also lectures on a variety of pop culture and historical subjects and teaches writing in the Connecticut area. He is the founder and Editor-in-Chief of the small press publishing company, The Stephen John Press, which recently published the acclaimed feminist autobiography, *Open Windows*.

Mr. Spignesi is a graduate of the University of New Haven and lives in New Haven, CT, with his wife, Pam, and their cat, Carter, named for their favorite character on *ER*.

Mr. Spignesi is currently writing an original requiem mass but requests that this not be interpreted to reflect on the state of his health or career.

Books by
Stephen J. Spignesi

- *Mayberry, My Hometown* (1987, Popular Culture, Ink).
- *The Complete Stephen King Encyclopedia* (1990, Contemporary Books).
- *The Stephen King Quiz Book* (1990, Signet).
- *The Second Stephen King Quiz Book* (1992, Signet).
- *The Woody Allen Companion* (1992, Andrews and McMeel).
- *The Official "Gone With the Wind" Companion* (1993, Plume).
- *The V. C. Andrews Trivia and Quiz Book* (1994, Signet).
- *The Odd Index: The Ultimate Compendium of Bizarre and Unusual Facts* (1994, Plume).
- *What's Your "Mad About You" IQ?* (1995, Citadel Press).
- *The Gore Galore Video Quiz Book* (1995, Signet).
- *What's Your "Friends" IQ?* (1996, Citadel Press).
- *The Celebrity Baby Name Book* (1996, Plume).
- *The "ER" Companion* (1996, Citadel Press).
- *J.F.K. Jr.* (1997, Citadel Press; originally titled *The J.F.K. Jr. Scrapbook*).

- *The Robin Williams Scrapbook* (1997, Citadel Press).
- *The Italian 100: A Ranking of the Most Influential Cultural, Scientific, and Political Figures, Past and Present* (1997, Citadel Press).
- *The Beatles Book of Lists* (1998, Citadel Press).
- *Young Kennedys: The New Generation* (1998, Avon; written as "Jay David Andrews").
- *The Lost Work Of Stephen King: A Guide to Unpublished Manuscripts, Story Fragments, Alternative Versions, & Oddities* (1998, Citadel Press).
- *The Complete Titanic: From the Ship's Earliest Blueprints to the Epic Film* (1998, Citadel Press).
- *Gems, Jewels, & Treasures* (2000, QVC Publishing) .
- *The USA Book of Lists* (2000, Career Press).
- *The Essential Stephen King: A Ranking of the 100 Greatest Novels, Short Stories, Movies, and Other Creations of the 20th Century's Reigning King of Horror* (2001, Career Press).
- *She Came in Through the Kitchen Window: Recipes Inspired by The Beatles & Their Music* (forthcoming).
- *The UFO Book of Lists* (forthcoming).
- *The Hollywood Book of Lists* (forthcoming).
- *Women in Bras* (unproduced screenplay).
- *Orchids* (unpublished novel).
- *Shelter Street* (novel-in-progress).